CHALLENGE

Intermediate Students' Book

SIMON HAINES and SIMON BREWSTER

CONTENTS

UNIT 1
Opener _____ 4
Stage one: Describing People _____ 5
Stage two: Occupations and Activities _____ 8
Activity: Character Analysis _____ 11
Language review _____ 12
    1 Quite and rather
    2 Age
    3 The Present Simple
    4 Frequency adverbs
    5 To look
    6 Comparative adjectives
    7 The Present Continuous

UNIT 2
Opener _____ 14
Stage one: Childhood Holidays _____ 15
Stage two: Nostalgia _____ 18
Activity: Mitchells Under Threat _____ 21
Language review _____ 22
    1 Used to
    2 The Past Simple
    3 Past time phrases
    4 Remember and forget
    5 Articles

UNIT 3
Opener _____ 23
Stage one: Describing Places _____ 24
Stage two: Describing Objects _____ 29
Activity: Holiday of a Lifetime _____ 31
Language review _____ 32
    1 Prepositions
    2 The definite article
    3 Describing objects
    4 Order of adjectives

UNIT 4
Opener _____ 33
Stage one: Leisure Activities _____ 34
Stage two: Favourite Things _____ 36
Activity: A Day in the Lake District _____ 38
Language review _____ 39
    1 Making suggestions
    2 Responding to suggestions
    3 Expressing likes and dislikes

UNIT 5
Opener _____ 40
Stage one: Relating Experiences _____ 41
Stage two: Dramatic Events _____ 44
Activity: Road Accident _____ 47
Language review _____ 49
    1 Sequencers
    2 The Present Perfect Simple
    3 Hear and see
    4 The Past Continuous

UNIT 6
Opener _____ 50
Stage one: Whose Health Is It Anyway? _____ 51
Stage two: Food Facts _____ 54
Activity: Burgers or Not? _____ 57
Language review _____ 58
    1 Asking for and giving opinions
    2 Agreeing and disagreeing
    3 Pronouns: you, we and they
    4 Compound pronouns

UNIT 7
Opener _____ 59
Stage one: Personal Experiences _____ 60
Stage two: Personal Details _____ 63
Activity: A Career in Books _____ 66
Language review _____ 68
    1 Question tags
    2 The Present Perfect Simple
    3 The Present Perfect Continuous
    4 The Present Perfect Simple and Continuous

UNIT 8
Opener _____ 69
Stage one: Views of the Future _____ 70
Stage two: Planning Ahead _____ 72
Activity: Are You an Optimist or a Pessimist? 76
Language review _____ 77
    1 The Future with will
    2 The Future Continuous
    3 The Future with going to and the Present Continuous
    4 Make and do

CONTENTS

UNIT 9
Opener 78
Stage one: Supermarket Shopping 79
Stage two: Valuables 82
Activity: Amusements? 84
Language review 85
    1 Some and any
    2 Prices, quantities and values
    3 Countable and uncountable nouns
    4 Many, much, a lot of
    5 Possessive adjectives and pronouns
    6 Object pronouns
    7 Measurements

UNIT 10
Opener 87
Stage one: Survival 88
Stage two: Life is Hard 91
Activity: School Rules 93
Language review 94
    1 Ability
    2 Can: summary of meanings
    3 Necessity
    4 Must or have to?
    5 Mustn't, needn't and don't have to

UNIT 11
Opener 95
Stage one: News Reports 96
Stage two: Messages and Excuses 99
Activity: Criminals Overheard 102
Language review 103
    1 Direct speech
    2 Reported speech
    3 Reporting verbs

UNIT 12
Opener 104
Stage one: People in Crisis 105
Stage two: Worries and Concerns 108
Activity: A Helping Hand 112
Language review 113
    1 Advice
    2 The First Conditional
    3 Superlative adjectives

UNIT 13
Opener 114
Stage one: Dangers and Uncertainties ... 115
Stage two: Possibilities 117
Activity: Soap Opera 120
Language review 122
    1 May and might
    2 Could
    3 How possible, how certain?
    4 Most

UNIT 14
Opener 123
Stage one: Wishful Thinking 124
Stage two: Recommendations 126
Activity: Advice for Travellers 130
Language review 131
    1 The Second Conditional
    2 Recommendations and obligations
    3 Articles

UNIT 15
Opener 132
Stage one: Moving Images 133
Stage two: What a Waste! 135
Activity: Let's Get Rid of It 138
Language review 140
    1 Passive verbs
    2 Expressing personal opinions

Communication Activities 141

Tapescripts 145

Irregular verbs 157

Index 158

Acknowledgements 160

UNIT 1

Opener

◆ Talk to your partner about these people. Who are they?

A

B

C

D

◆ Choose the correct caption for each photo.

• Diana Ross	• Elvis Presley	• Meryl Streep
• Clark Gable	• Professional Impersonator	• Princess Diana
• Roy Orbison	• Humphrey Bogart	• Tina Turner

◆ Who do the four people look like? *(to look like = to resemble)*
   EXAMPLE: *C looks like Humphrey Bogart.*

◆ Fill in this table with adjectives which describe their appearance.

	Hair	Eyes	Expression	Clothes
A	black			
B		?		
C				formal
D			happy	

page 4   UNIT 1 Opener

Stage one

Describing People

1 Listening

Look at these photographs of young people studying in Britain. Listen to the people talking about themselves and match the descriptions with the photos.

☐ ☐ ☐ ☐ ☐

● **Listening for detail**

Listen again and fill in the details in this table.

Name	Age	Occupation	Nationality	Eyes	Hair	Height
1 Yolanda	21					X
2 Ali		student		X		
3 Simone		X		X		quite tall
4 Miguel			Bolivian			
5 Dolores				greyish		

(X = *The speakers do not give this information.*)

2 Vocabulary

● **Opposites**

Match these adjectives with their opposites:

a tall
b wavy/curly
c short
d dark
e slim
f short-sighted
g thin

• long-sighted
• short
• fat/plump
• long
• thick
• straight
• fair/pale

● **Adjectives with *-ish***

Dolores says her eyes are *greyish*. This means they are quite grey or a mixture of grey and another colour.

Describe the colour of these eyes using *-ish* words:

UNIT 1 Stage one page 5

Add -ish to other words to describe the people in the photograph.

EXAMPLES: *The man is about 40. He's fortyish.*
The woman is tallish and slim.

● **Nationality**

EXAMPLE: *Simone is French. She comes from France.*

Make a sentence like this about yourself.

Make similar sentences about internationally famous people.

3 Quite and rather
(Language review 1, page 12)

Quite and *rather* both mean 'not very' but 'more than a little'.

EXAMPLES: *She's quite an intelligent person.*
I'm rather short for a man.

Do you think *quite* and *rather* have positive or negative meanings?

Describe one of your friends using *quite*, *rather* and *very*.

4 Practice

Read this short description:

Leyton Summers is 53 years old. He has long black hair and he's rather plump. He's a professional Elvis Presley impersonator, so he wears bright colourful clothes.

Write a short description of someone in your English class. (Don't mention their name.)

Read or show your sentences to other students – they have to guess who you have described.

page 6   UNIT 1 Stage one

5 Regular actions and statements that are always true
(Language review 3, page 12)

Read these comments that Yolanda, the first speaker, made about herself:

I'm 21 and I come from Spain. I work in a hotel as a receptionist. I've got dark curly hair and brown eyes. My face is round. What else can I say about myself? I have to look my best for work, so I usually wear make-up – but not too much.

What have all the verbs got in common? Discuss your ideas with a partner.

Now read these comments that other speakers made. Decide whether each one refers to a regular action (a habit) or to something that is always true. Put RA or AT in each box.

1 I come from Algeria. ☐
2 I'm quite tall for a girl. ☐
3 I usually wear my hair tied back. ☐
4 I'm French. ☐
5 I don't often wear make-up. ☐
6 I prefer to look natural. ☐
7 I sometimes wear glasses. ☐
8 I live in Bolivia. ☐
9 I speak two languages. ☐

6 Pairwork
(Language review 2, page 12)

Write short descriptions of yourself and your partner. Mention these points: age, occupation, nationality, height, hair, eyes, and clothes.

Compare your descriptions and discuss the differences.

7 Pronunciation

The ending of the *he/she/it* form of the Present Simple has three different sounds:

a) plays /z/   b) gets /s/   c) watches /ɪz/

Listen to the verbs in the Present Simple in this short dialogue. Which of the three endings do they have?

1 does /   /   6 goes /   /
2 catches /   / 7 makes /   /
3 looks /   /   8 reads /   /
4 meets /   /   9 watches /   /
5 stays /   /   10 gets /   /

8 How often?
(Language review 4, page 12)

Underline the words or phrases in these sentences which tell you how often something happens. The first one has been done for you.

1 She usually gets up at 8 o'clock.
2 I hardly ever listen to the radio.
3 My mother never drinks coffee in the evening.
4 My father always reads the newspaper in the morning.
5 I sometimes play football at the weekend.
6 Yolanda often wears earrings.
7 Dolores occasionally writes letters.

Now put the words and phrases into descending order of frequency. The first and the last have been given.

1 always 2 u 3 o
4 s 5 oc 6 He
7 never

What can you say about the position of these words in their sentences? Compare you ideas with a partner.

How many other 'how often' words or phrases do you know?

EXAMPLES: *every day   once a week*

Write five sentences about yourself using some of these 'frequency' words and phrases.

9 Survey of routines

Work in groups of four and ask each other these questions:

How often do you ...

1 ... play football?
2 ... write a letter?
3 ... read a book?
4 ... get up late?

Now ask each other some more questions.

11 Vocabulary
(Language review 5 and 6, page 13)

Read the text again and find:

a five family words (e.g. *husband*)
b five job or occupation words (e.g. *teacher*)
c five different verbs in the Present Simple.

Describe and compare the two brothers.

Make up sentences like these:

*John and David both look very friendly.
John looks younger than David, but actually he's two years older than his brother.
David looks like an actor.*

10 Reading

Read this text about John and David Suchet. As you read, find three differences between the two brothers.

John Suchet, 46, was for many years a reporter, and now presents ITN's *News at One* on ITV. He has three sons, Damian, 19, Kieran, 16, and Rory, 15, by his first marriage. He and his second wife, Bonnie, live in Baker Street. His parents, Jack and Joan Suchet, live in the same block. Actor David Suchet, 43, was a member of the Royal Shakespeare Company for 12 years. His television credits include *Poirot, Freud, Blott On The Landscape* and *Song For Europe*. He is married to actress Sheila Ferris and they have a son, Robert, nine, and daughter, Catherine, seven. They live in west London. John and David have a younger brother, Peter, aged 37, an advertising executive.

12 Writing

Write about someone you know very well – for example, your best friend or someone in your family. Describe the person and then compare yourself to him or her.

EXAMPLE: *My best friend is called Maria. She's tall and has long blond hair. She looks like a film star, but actually she's a student. She looks older than me, but we're the same age.*

UNIT 1 Stage one page 7

Stage two

Occupations and Activities

1 Listening

The presenter of a weekly television chat show is introducing two of his guests.

As you listen, make notes about the guests' occupations. Do they have anything in common with each other?

● **Listening for detail**

Listen to the interviews again and then say whether these statements are true or false. Circle the letter T or F.

1 David Conolly is an environmentalist.	T/F
2 He teaches at Oxford University.	T/F
3 He sometimes works as a television presenter.	T/F
4 He is making a television programme about British night-life.	T/F
5 He is trying to protect animals, birds and plants.	T/F
6 Danielle Davidson is an American singer.	T/F
7 This is her first visit to London.	T/F
8 She says the traffic in London is worse than it is in New York.	T/F
9 Every day she is on stage for more than two hours without a break.	T/F
10 She doesn't get up very early in the morning.	T/F

2 Prepositions

Fill the gaps in these sentences with suitable prepositions from the list. (You can use the prepositions more than once.)

Listen to the recording for Exercise 1 again. Listen carefully for phrases with prepositions like those in sentences 1-7. Check your answers with the tapescript on page 145.

about   at   by   for   from   in   into   on   with

1 Harrison Ford is best known _____ his role as the archaeologist Indiana Jones in *Raiders of the Lost Ark*.

2 More and more people have an interest _____ environmental protection.

3 These days, politicians frequently appear _____ television.

4 Are you watching the new TV series _____ food and health?

5 The world is changing _____ an increasingly fast rate.

6 A few years ago, Dustin Hoffman appeared _____ a Shakespeare play in London.

7 _____ the end of an evening show, most actors go straight to bed.

page **8** UNIT 1 Stage two

3 Regular actions or temporary activities
(Language review 7, page 13)

Here are two extracts from the interview with David Connolly:

*David Connolly teaches at Cambridge University.
He is making a television series about wildlife in Britain.*

What is the difference between these two sentences? Compare your ideas with a partner.

Look at some more extracts from the interviews. Do they refer to a regular action or to a temporary activity? Put RA or TA in each box.

1 David Connolly writes books. ☐
2 He appears regularly on television. ☐
3 What are you doing these days? ☐
4 We're losing rare animals, birds and plants. ☐
5 Danielle Davidson is appearing in Starshine. ☐
6 I'm enjoying the show. ☐
7 I'm getting a little tired. ☐
8 I get up late. ☐
9 I take it easy during the day. ☐

4 Pairwork

Make a list of some of the activities you are currently involved in.

EXAMPLES:
Leisure: *I'm playing in the school tennis competition.*
School work: *I'm revising for the end-of-year exams.*
Job: *I'm planning a new advertising campaign.*

Ask questions to find out what activities your partner is involved in.

EXAMPLE:
You: *I think you're playing for the school football team, aren't you?*
Partner: *No, I'm not. I'm playing in the tennis tournament.*

5 Things that are happening now
(Language review 7, page 13)

Look at this picture. Fill in the words missing from the second bubble:

What do you think is happening in these pictures? Write down your ideas.

Compare your ideas with other students.

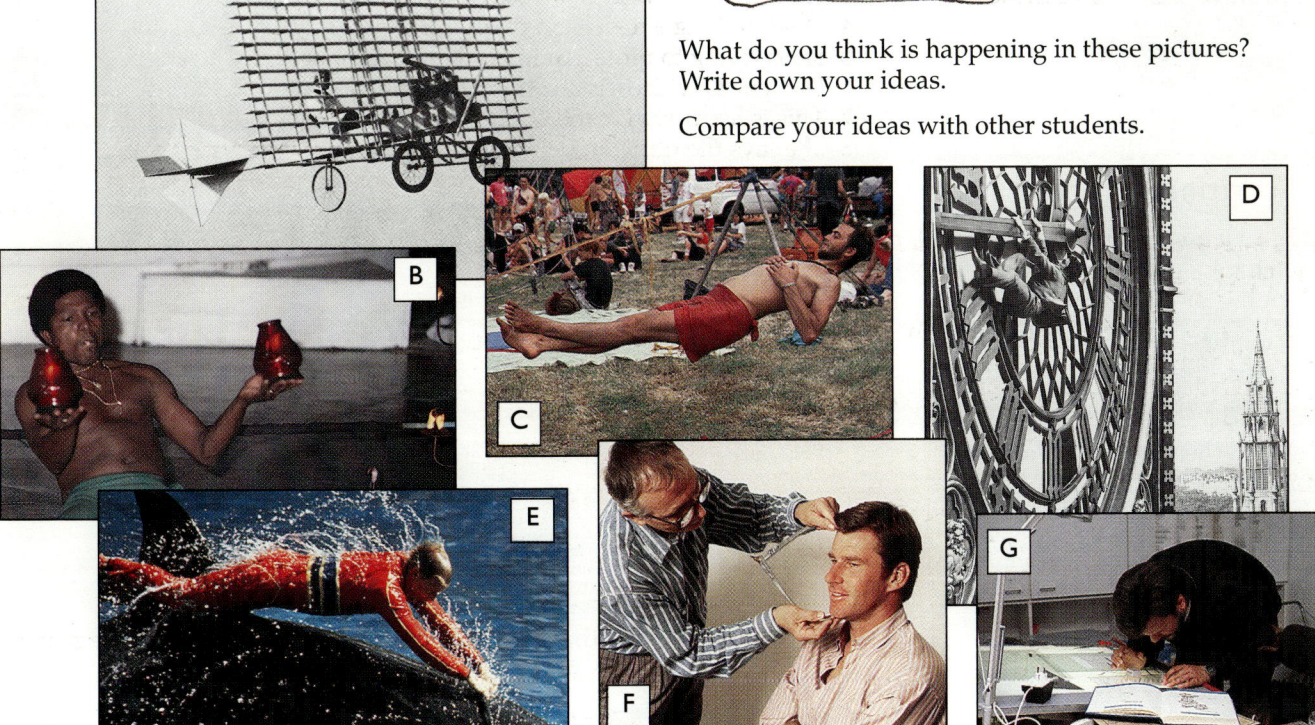

UNIT 1 Stage two   page 9

6 Reading

What is the writer of this letter doing in Brazil? Read and find out.

Make a list of all the present tense verbs in this letter. Write the verbs under the following headings:

1 Regular actions or things that are always true.

   EXAMPLES:
   The sun shines every day.
   The Rio Palace overlooks Copacabana Beach.

2 Activities that the writer is involved in.

   EXAMPLE:
   I'm spending a week here.

3 Things that are happening now.

   EXAMPLE:
   I'm writing this letter on my hotel balcony.

How do you think this letter continues? Discuss your ideas with a partner.

RIO PALACE

Monday 17th September

Dear Josey,

I'm spending a week here at an international trade conference. We're discussing how poor countries can cut their inflation rates and raise the living standards of ordinary people.

Rio is fantastic! The weather is incredible – the sun shines every day, and it hardly ever rains. The people here are really friendly and relaxed. They enjoy everything they do and always seem happy. The music is wonderful, too. I'd love to come back here at Carnival time.

I'm writing this letter on my hotel balcony. The Rio Palace overlooks Copacabana Beach. It's only 10 o'clock in the morning, and the beach is already crowded. Hundreds of people are swimming and sunbathing, and lots of boys are playing football. Everyone loves football here. That's about the only thing that the people in Manchester and the people ...

7 Writing: informal letters

Write a letter to someone you haven't seen for a long time. Here is a sample layout.

Tell your friend about your present situation, and some of the activities you are involved in.

Tell him/her about your current routine.

Tell him/her what is happening where you are at the moment – while you are writing this letter.

	16, Chaucer Way Cambridge CB2 0KL	Your address
	25.7.91	Date
Beginnings:	Dear Mike Dearest Mike (My) darling Mike	friendly very friendly intimate
Endings:	Best wishes/All the best Love/With love and best wishes All my love	friendly very friendly intimate

page 10　UNIT 1 Stage two

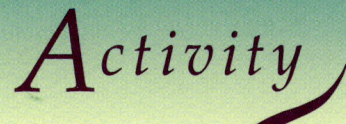

Character Analysis

1 Discussion
Work in groups of three or four.

What do you know about these ways of finding out about someone's character?

Graphology   Phrenology   Palmistry   Astrology

Do you know any other ways?

What do you think of these 'sciences'? Discuss your ideas with your partners.

2 Writing and discussion
Work in pairs.

Write a short description of your partner's character.

EXAMPLES: *She's very direct. She always says what she thinks.
She's a sociable person and has a lot of friends.*

Read what your partner has written about you. Do you think it is an accurate description of your character?

3 Doodles
Work in pairs.

A doodle is a drawing or pattern that you do when you are bored or when you are thinking about something else.

You are going to find out about your partner's character by studying his/her doodles. Here are some typical doodles:

Try to find an old doodle. Look in your exercise book or your diary. If you can't find one, do one quickly now.

Exchange doodles with your partner. What do you think the doodle tells you about your partner's character?

Turn to page 141 and read the description of the kind of person who does doodles like this.

Language review

1 Quite and rather

Quite and *rather* mean 'not very, but more than a little'.

Use *quite* with positive ideas:

> I'm **quite** tall.
> (The speaker thinks it is good to be tall.)

Use *rather* with negative or surprising ideas:

> You're **rather** late.
> (The speaker thinks it is not good to be late.)
> I don't like television chat shows, but this one was **rather** interesting.

Notice the position of *quite* and *rather* in these sentences:

> I'm **quite** intelligent.
> I'm **quite** an intelligent person.
> It's **rather** cold today.
> It's **rather** a cold day or It's a **rather** cold day.

2 Age

Use these expressions to talk about how old people are:

> How old are you?
> I'm 23 (years old).
> I'm nearly 17.
> I'm just 19. (= I am 19 and a few days or weeks)
> He's a 50-year-old British actor. (notice the hyphens)
> She's in her mid-twenties/late thirties/early forties.
> My teacher is about 53 years old.
> He's fiftyish.

3 The Present Simple

In this unit the Present Simple is used

a) to talk about regular actions or habits
   I usually wear make-up.
   Miguel sometimes plays football.

b) to talk about things that are always true:
   I come from Algeria.
   My skin is pale and my eyes are greyish.

● **Notes on the form of the Present Simple**

The *I, you, we* and *they* forms of the Present Simple of most verbs is the same as the infinitive:

> come   I come
> live   you live
> speak we speak
> wear   they wear

For the *he, she* and *it* form we add *-s*:

> come   he comes
> live   she lives
> depend it depends

Questions and negative forms use the auxiliary verbs *do/does* and *don't/doesn't*:

> Does Thomas play tennis?
> She doesn't speak Russian.

A few common verbs have irregular Present Simple forms:

> be   I am
>   you/we/they are
>   he/she/it is
> have he has
> do   she does
> go   he goes

Modal verbs do not have the extra *-s* in the *he/she/it* form:

> I can   he can
> you must   she must
> we should   it should

4 Frequency adverbs

Frequency adverbs are words which tell us how often something happens. (We use them with the Present Simple not the Present Continuous.)

> always usually often sometimes occasionally
> hardly ever never

Notice the position of the frequency adverbs in these sentences:

> I **hardly ever** listen to the radio.
> Ali **sometimes** plays golf.
> Yolanda doesn't **often** get up late.
> Do you **usually** walk to work?

Usually, often, sometimes and *occasionally* can also be used to start positive sentences:

> **Usually** I start work at 9 o'clock.
> **Sometimes** I start at 8 o'clock.

Here are some more ways of saying how often something happens:

once (twice/three times etc.) + a period of time:

> I go to London **twice a year**.
> I see my parents **three times a week**.

every + period of time:

> I go to work **every day**.
> I go to the dentist **every six months**.

page 12 | UNIT 1 Language review

5 To look

Notice these different meanings of the verb *to look*:

a) *to look at something*:
I looked **at my watch**. It was already half-past four.

b) *to look + adjective*:
You look **tired and pale**. Are you alright?

c) *to look like + noun*:
He looks **like a politician**, but actually he's a car salesman.

6 Comparative adjectives

To compare two things or people, use the comparative form of adjectives with *than*:

Steve looks **younger than** Mike.
Steve is actually two years **older than** his brother.

Here are some other comparative forms:

a) Double the last consonant:
big *bigger*   thin *thinner*   hot *hotter*

b) Change *-y* to *-i*:
happy *happier*   heavy *heavier*

c) Add only *-r*:
late *later*   pale *paler*

d) Use *more* with long adjectives:
interesting *more interesting*
intelligent *more intelligent*

e) Irregular comparative forms:
good *better*   bad *worse*

7 The Present Continuous

In this unit the Present Continuous is used to talk about temporary activities which are happening around the time of speaking:

What are you doing these days?
I'm making a new television series about wildlife in Britain.
Danielle is appearing in the American musical Starshine.

It is also used to talk about things that are happening at the moment of speaking:

A 'Is your mother busy?'
B 'Yes, I'm afraid she is. She's talking to someone on the phone at the moment.'
A 'And your father?'
B 'He's eating his lunch.'

Some verbs are hardly ever used in the Present Continuous. Here are a few examples:

'Liking' verbs: *like love prefer*
'Knowing' verbs: *believe know remember understand*
Other verbs: *want need hear see seem*

Here are some common time adverbs used with the Present Continuous:

At the moment *I'm writing a new book.*
She's **currently** *working in New York.*
What are you doing **these days**?

UNIT 2
Opener

◆ Look at this photograph of Piccadilly Circus in London, and discuss these questions with your partner:

1 What are the people in the photograph doing?
2 What can you say about the methods of transport?
3 When do you think this photo was taken?
4 How would a photo of Piccadilly Circus taken in the 1990s be different?

Stage one

Childhood Holidays

1 Listening 🎧

Listen to these three people talking about their holidays.

As you listen, match the holiday photos with the speakers' memories.

● **Listening for detail**

Listen to the cassette again. Where did the speakers go for their holidays when they were children and where do they go now?

	When they were children	Now
Speaker 1	S. Wales	Cyprus/France
Speaker 2	Ireland	World/Portugal
Speaker 3	Brighton	Spain

Answer these questions:
1. How long did it take the first speaker to travel from London to South Wales?
2. Where did the family stay in South Wales?
3. How long did the second speaker's holidays in Ireland last?
4. How did the third speaker and his family travel to Brighton?
5. Why did they stop going there?

2 Vocabulary

● **Meanings**

Look at the tapescript for Exercise 1 on page 145. Find words which mean about the same as:

1 members of the same family: _____

2 bags, suitcases etc: _____

3 travelling around a place to get to know it: _____

4 to do things but with no particular purpose or plan: to _____ around

5 high class: _____

● **Phrases with numbers**

The first speaker's train journey to South Wales took 8 hours.
It was an *eight-hour* journey.
The third speaker didn't stay in an expensive hotel.
It wasn't a *five-star* hotel.

Make some more hyphenated phrases like these. The first one has been done for you.

1 I went on a course which lasted three weeks.
   It was a *three-week* course.

2 Our house has three storeys. It's a _____ house.

3 We spoke for 30 minutes on the telephone.
   We had a _____ telephone conversation.

4 The family next door have two cars. They're a _____ _____.

5 This motorway has five lanes. It's a _____ _____.

6 Last year we spent six days on holiday in the south of France. We had a _____ _____.

UNIT 2 Stage one   page 15

3 Transport

What are the names of these types of transport?

Now fill in the gaps in these sentences with one of these three prepositions:

by   in   on

1 My father went to work _____ a steam train.
2 I like travelling _____ plane.
3 I go to school _____ my bike.
4 Last year we had a holiday _____ a camper van.
5 I hate travelling _____ bus.
6 It's dangerous to ride _____ the back of a motorbike.
7 My parents go everywhere _____ car.
8 I'd love to go somewhere _____ a helicopter.

4 Talking about the past
(Language review 1 and 2, page 22)

This is part of what the first speaker said. Read it carefully and underline the words or phrases which show that the speaker spent more than one holiday in South Wales.

'We used to go to relatives in South Wales, and going there on the steam train was really exciting. It was an eight-hour journey from London, and my father was always late …'

Now read these sentences and decide whether they refer to a single or a repeated action. Put S or R in each box.

1 We always rented a large house near the beach. ☐ R
2 One year we went to Cornwall. ☐ S
3 I loved our trips to Bournemouth. ☐ R
4 In 1969 we went to the Channel Islands. ☐ S
5 Until I was nearly thirteen we went to Spain. ☐ R
6 We used to stay in small family hotels. ☐ R
7 When we went to Brighton it always rained. ☐ R
8 I'll never forget our visit to New York. ☐ S

5 Past time phrases
(Language review 3, page 22)

Listen again to the three people talking about their holidays.

Make a list of the time phrases they use.

EXAMPLE: *In those days* (it was an eight-hour journey from London).

6 Pronunciation

The Past Simple of regular verbs always ends in -ed:

play *played*   watch *watched*   start *started*

but the -ed ending can have 3 different sounds:

played /d/   *started* /ɪd/   *watched* /t/

Listen for these three words in this short conversation.

Now listen to a telephone conversation between Sue and Annie. How do they say these verbs? Tick the correct column.

	/d/ (played)	/ɪd/ (started)	/t/ (watched)
1 visited			
2 moved			
3 stayed			
4 wanted			
5 rained			
6 decided			
7 missed			
8 cleaned			
9 finished			
10 started			

UNIT 2 Stage one

7 Holiday survey

How did you spend your holidays when you were a child? Work in groups of four and fill in a chart like this, first for yourself and then for three partners.

Ask questions, using the prompts below.

EXAMPLE: *Where did you use to go for your holidays?*

	Yourself	Partner 1	Partner 2	Partner 3
1 Where/go?				
2 How/travel?				
3 How long/stay?				
4 Who/go with?				
5 Where/stay?				

Now fill in a similar chart about how you and your partners spend your holidays now.

Compare the notes you have made with the notes of another group. Can you make any generalisations about holiday trends?

Write sentences like this:

Most people used to travel by _____, but now they …

8 Memories
(Language review 4, page 22)

What is your earliest childhood memory? Is it more like Simon's or Anne's? Read and find out.

Simon
I can remember going to hospital with scarlet fever. It was an isolation hospital – that meant that no visitors were allowed inside the building. I'll never forget talking to my Mum and Dad through the closed window. I always cried when they left. Lots of people bought me presents, but I couldn't take them home with me when I left. I was only about four years old.

Anne
I remember my first bike. I got it on my fifth birthday. In those days you didn't use to know what presents you were going to get. It was a Sunday, so I didn't have to go to school. I'll never forget how I felt when I woke up and saw this strange-shaped package next to my bed. At first I was quite frightened – it looked like a monster.

Think about your earliest memories. As you start to remember people, places and events, write notes like this:

1. First day at school
2. 5th birthday: presents/party
3. First time I saw snow

Compare memories with a partner.

9 Writing

Write fuller notes about one of your childhood memories.

EXAMPLE:

First day at school
Me - 4½ years old / best clothes
Getting there - Dad's car
School - very big / lots of people / no friends / kind teacher - Miss Wright

Now expand your notes into a full story of about 100 words.

Stage two

Nostalgia

1 Reading

This strip cartoon traces the history of a building. The people who live in the area remember the changes with mixed feelings.

How many different uses has the building had? Look at the cartoon to find out.

Remember when it was the Rose and Crown?

It was always full of noisy men who drank too much.

And you waited 10 minutes before you got a drink.

Never anywhere to sit.

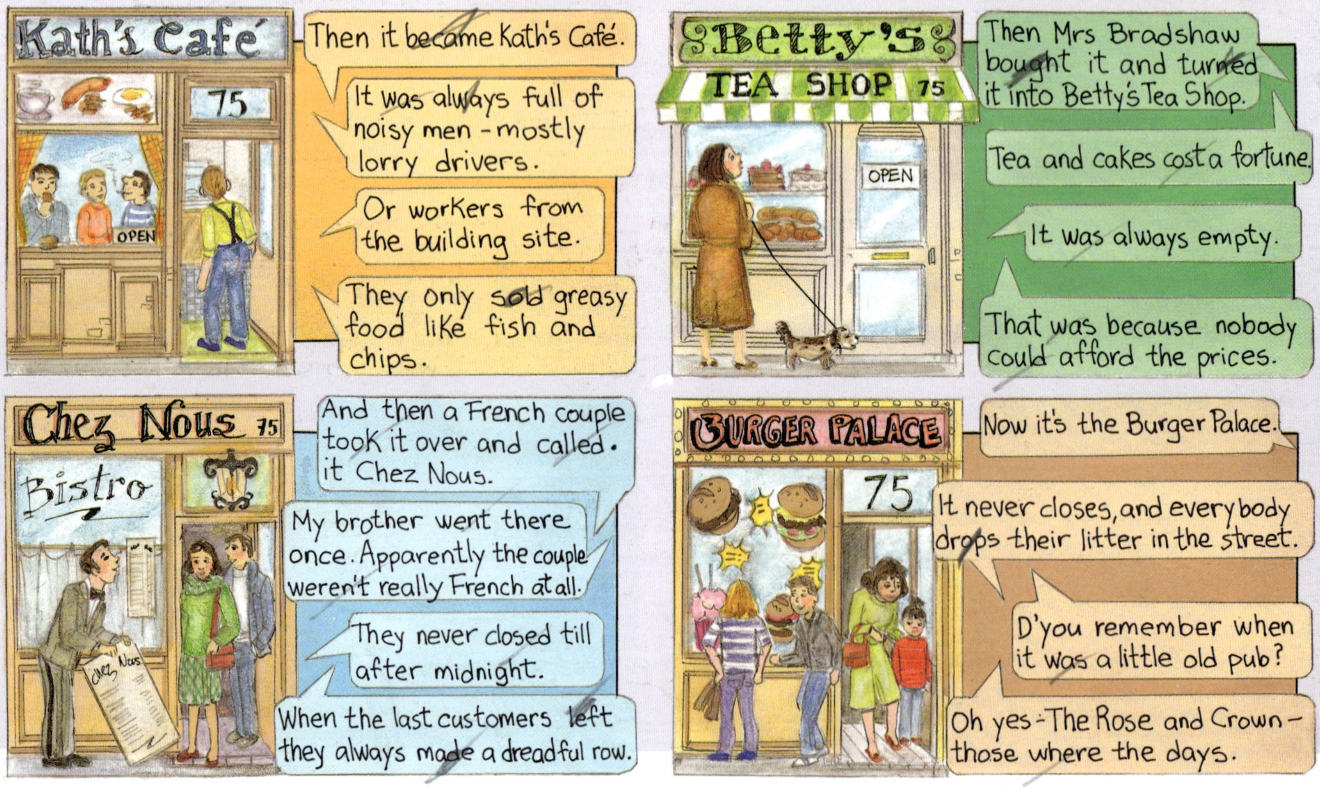

Then it became Kath's Café.

It was always full of noisy men – mostly lorry drivers.

Or workers from the building site.

They only sold greasy food like fish and chips.

Then Mrs Bradshaw bought it and turned it into Betty's Tea Shop.

Tea and cakes cost a fortune.

It was always empty.

That was because nobody could afford the prices.

And then a French couple took it over and called it Chez Nous.

My brother went there once. Apparently the couple weren't really French at all.

They never closed till after midnight.

When the last customers left they always made a dreadful row.

Now it's the Burger Palace.

It never closes, and everybody drops their litter in the street.

D'you remember when it was a little old pub?

Oh yes – The Rose and Crown – those where the days.

page 18   UNIT 2 Stage two

● **Reading for detail**

Fill in this chart with as many details as you can about the building at different times. Some answers have been given for you.

Why are the speakers complaining about the building? Write a list of the complaints.

EXAMPLE:

1 *The pub was full of noisy men; they drank too much; customers had to wait a long time for a drink.*

	Name	Use	Owners	Things sold
1	The Rose & Crown			
2		café		
3			Mrs Bradshaw	
4	Chez Nous			
5				

2 Vocabulary

Match these words from the cartoon with their meanings:

1 to afford — a to be very expensive
2 greasy — b people said
3 to turn into — c things were better in the past
4 to cost a fortune — d oily
5 to take over — e to be very noisy
6 apparently — f to change, make different
7 to make a row — g to have the money to pay for
8 those were the days — h to become the owner (to buy)

3 Talking points

Discuss these points with a partner:

1 Why do buildings like the one in the cartoon change so often?
2 What sort of people are the four speakers?
3 Why do they complain about the building?

4 A or the?
(Language review 5, page 22)

Here are two sentences from the cartoon:

Then a French couple took it over …
Apparently the couple weren't really French at all.

What is the difference between: **a French couple** and **the couple**?
Compare ideas with a partner.

5 Listening

Listen to a recorded version of the 'Good Old Days' conversation. There are nine differences between the recording and the cartoon text. Listen carefully and make a list of these differences.

EXAMPLE:

		Cartoon	Recording
Frame 1	(a)	drank	ate
	(b)	got	
Frame 2	(c)		

6 Talking about the past
(Language review 2, page 22)

Make a list of all the past tense verbs in the cartoon. Next to each verb write its base form.

Are these verbs regular or irregular? Write R or I.

EXAMPLE:

Past	Base form	R or I
1 was	be	I
2 waited	wait	
3 got		

7 Phrasal verbs: take

*That Frenchman **took it over*** means:
That Frenchman bought the building and started to run it (as a business).

Work out the meanings of the 'take' verbs in these sentences.

Then rewrite the sentences replacing the verbs.

1 The factory took on a hundred new workers last year.
2 She invited me to lunch and I took her up on her offer.
3 My sister only started playing the piano a month ago, but she took to it immediately.
4 I'm sorry for what I said. I take it all back. *withdraws*
5 He's always so busy at work. He never takes any time off. *(holiday)*

8 Towns past and present

Look at this photograph of a British town. When do you think it was taken? How was life different in those days? Make a list of differences.

Compare lists with a partner.

Now discuss what life was like in your town or city 10 or 20 years ago.

~ What was better and what was worse in those days?
~ What did people look like? Think about hairstyles and fashions.
~ What did people do in their spare time?
~ What sort of music was popular then?

Activity

Mitchells Under Threat

1 Reading

This article is on the front page of a British newspaper. What is it about?
Read the headline, look at the photograph, and then make a guess.
Now read the text to see if your guess was right.

The Globe asks "Do we really need another office block in Kingsworth?"

Family shop to make way for yuppie office block

London property developer Mr David Wattis is seeking planning permission to knock down Mitchells General Store in Queen Street and put up a 15-storey office in its place. The general store has served the community for more than 100 years and is popular with local people.

Mitchells: "Still popular after 100 years."

2 Writing

Work in pairs.

Student A: Turn to page 141.
Student B: Read these instructions:

- You use Mitchells regularly, and you are very annoyed about the plan to knock the shop down to make way for an office block. If the shop disappears, you will have to catch a bus to the nearest supermarket.

- Write a letter to the editor of The Globe. Explain why you disapprove of the plan. Start like this:

```
                                          Your address
The Editor,
The Globe,
High Street,
Kingsworth
                                          Date
Dear Sir,
I was very angry when I read your lead story last week about the
plan to replace Mitchells with an office block. I must say ...

Yours faithfully,

               (Signature)
Name in capitals
```

3 Reading and discussion

Exchange letters with your partner. Read and discuss each other's points of view.

Language review

1 Used to

In this unit *used to* + the infinitive describes:

a) past routines - regular events and activities which no longer happen:

   We used to go to relatives in South Wales.
   We used to go to Scotland every year; now we always go abroad.

b) past situations which are no longer true:

   It used to be a pretty little shop.

● **Notes on the form of *used to***

Used to has the same form for all persons:

   I used to, he used to, etc.

Questions and negative forms have *use*, not *used*:

   *Where did you **use** to go for your holidays?*
   *We didn't **use** to go abroad every year.*

Do not confuse *used to* + infinitive with *to be used to* + *-ing* form:

   I used to walk on the beach. = This was an old habit or routine.
   I'm used to walking fast. = I am accustomed to walking fast.

2 The Past Simple

In this unit the Past Simple is used to describe:

a) finished past actions:

   My aunt gave me a teapot for Christmas.

b) actions which lasted for a length of time, but are now completed:

   When I was a child, we lived on the south coast of England.

c) repeated past actions:

   We (always) went by car. (This means the same as *We used to go by car.*)

● **Notes on the form of the Past Simple**

a) The Past Simple has the same form for all persons.

   Questions and negative forms use the auxiliary verbs *did* and *didn't*:

   'When did you arrive?'
   'We didn't arrive until last night.'

b) The Simple Past of all regular verbs ends in *-ed*:

   look - *looked*;   play - *played*;   discover - *discovered*

c) But notice these variations in spelling:

1 Double the last letter of short verbs if the infinitive has one vowel (*a, e, i, o, u*) and ends in one consonant (*n, p, t* etc):

   plan - *planned*;   stop - *stopped*;   fit - *fitted*

2 Add only the letter *-d* if the infinitive ends in *-e*:

   like - *liked*;   love - *loved*;   decide - *decided*

3 Change *y* to *ie* if the infinitive ends in a consonant + *y*:

   cry - *cried*;   carry - *carried*;   spy - *spied*

● **Irregular verbs**

Many common verbs in English are irregular in the Past Simple. Here are a few of the examples from this unit:

   be *was/were*   do *did*   eat *ate*
   have *had*   go *went*   make *made*

There is a complete list of irregular verbs on page 157.

3 Past time phrases

Notice these time phrases which are used in Unit 2:

   Last year we spent time exploring Provence.
   The year before last I went to Portugal to play golf.
   At that time nobody went abroad.
   When I was a child we lived on the south coast.
   In those days it was an eight-hour journey from London.

4 Remember and forget

When we are talking about memories the verbs *remember* and *forget* can be followed by nouns, *-ing* form verbs or clauses.

1 noun: *I (can)* remember one particular Christmas.*

2 -ing form: *I (can)* remember getting my first bike.*

3 clause: *I'll never forget how I felt when I woke up and saw this strange-shaped package next to my bed.*

**Note: can* is often used with *remember*.

5 Articles

When we first mention something, we use *a*:

   *My aunt gave me **a** teapot for Christmas.*

When we mention the same thing again, we use *the*:

   *I remember **the** teapot very well, but ...*

page 22   UNIT 2 Language review

UNIT 3 Opener

◆ Where is this city?

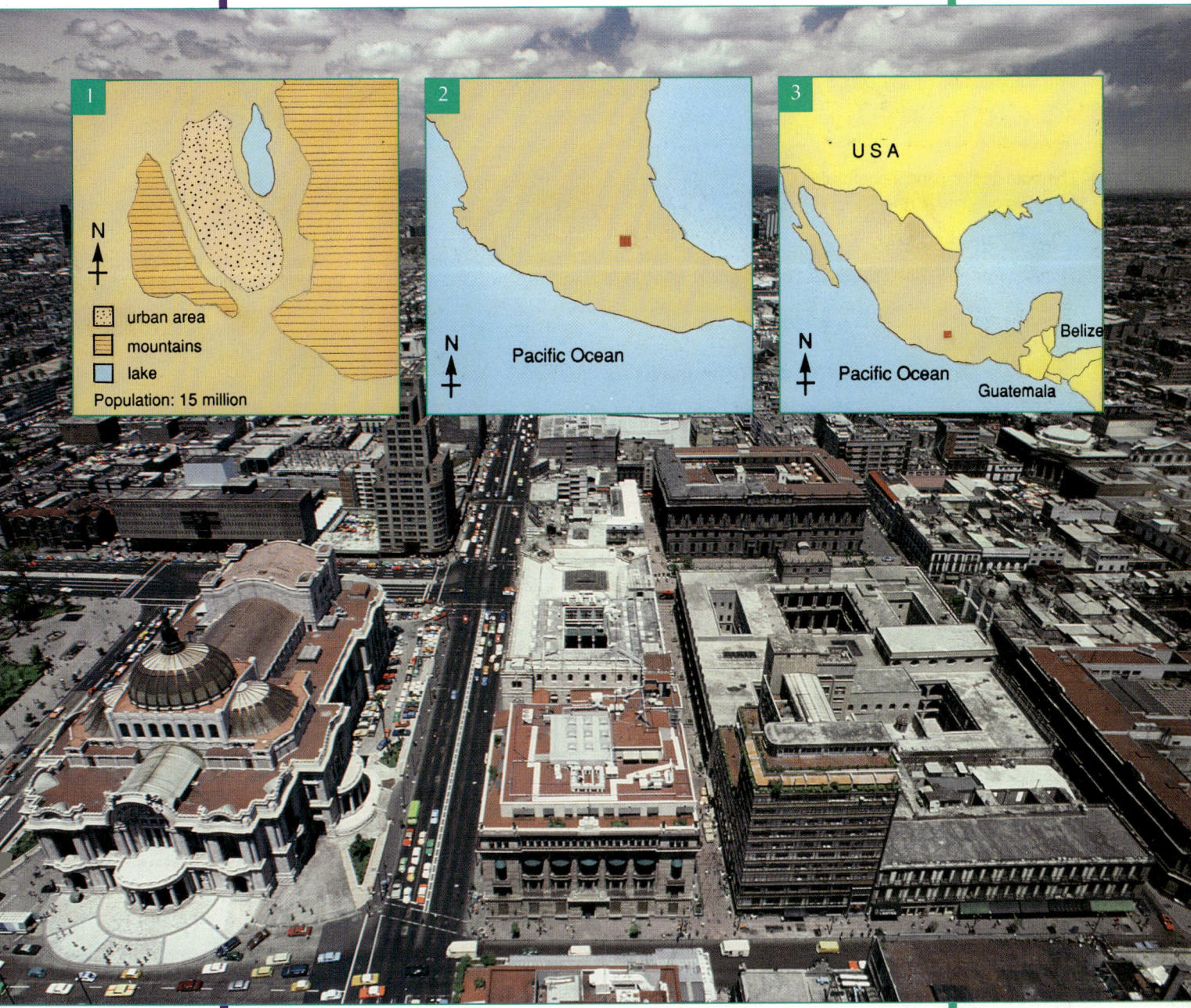

◆ Look carefully at the three maps and with your partner say as much as you can about each one. You should try to include:

1 The city's position and population.
2 Its geographical location.
3 Some information about where the country is.

◆ Can you identify the city and the country?

Describing Places

1 Reading

Read these three extracts. What sort of texts do you think they are taken from?

1 Coventry is a modern industrial city with a population of 333,000.

2 Well Angela. Here we are on the west coast!

3 The train had crossed a peninsula, from Hakodate to Mori.

● **Understanding**

Read Text 1. What sort of city is Coventry?

Now pick a city in your own country which is similar to Coventry. Note the similarities between both cities. Compare your information with another student.

Use these headings to help you:

Name: _____

Population: _____

Geographical position: _____

Nearest airport: _____

Famous for: _____

Nearby places of interest: _____

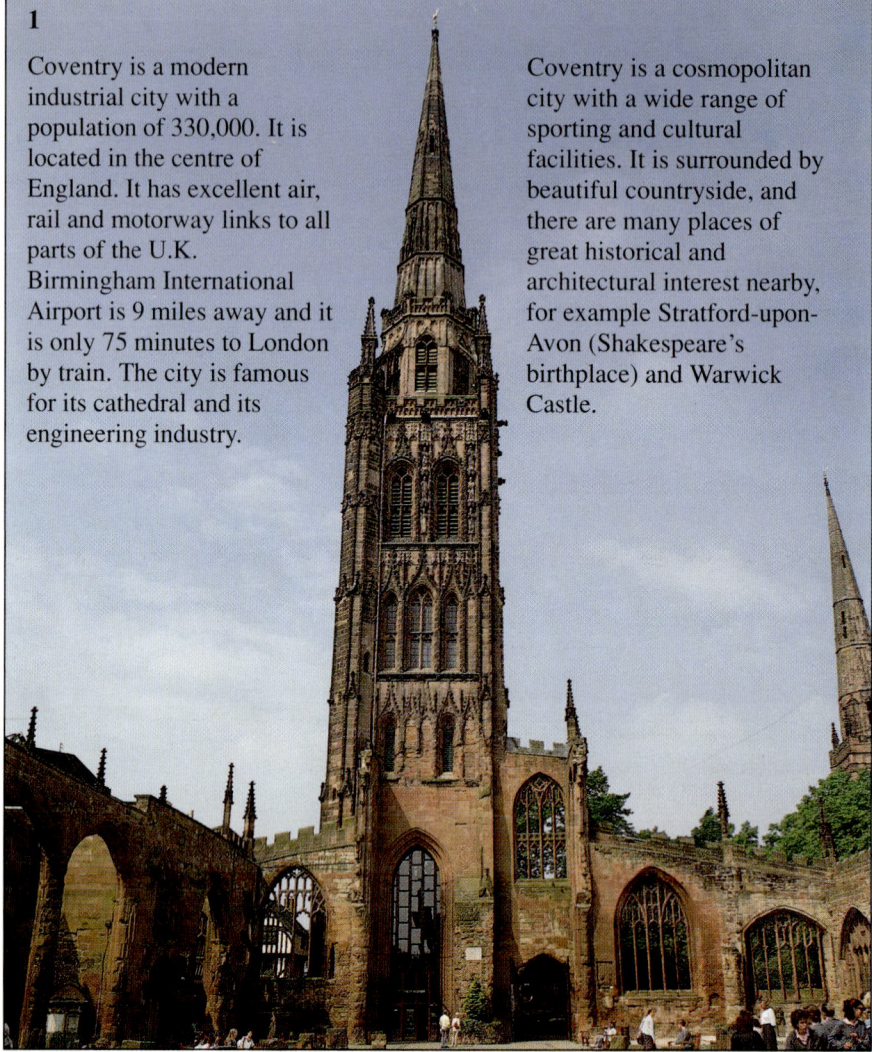

1

Coventry is a modern industrial city with a population of 330,000. It is located in the centre of England. It has excellent air, rail and motorway links to all parts of the U.K. Birmingham International Airport is 9 miles away and it is only 75 minutes to London by train. The city is famous for its cathedral and its engineering industry.

Coventry is a cosmopolitan city with a wide range of sporting and cultural facilities. It is surrounded by beautiful countryside, and there are many places of great historical and architectural interest nearby, for example Stratford-upon-Avon (Shakespeare's birthplace) and Warwick Castle.

2 Vocabulary

Look at the sentences and for each one choose a suitable adjective from the list which combines with the other adjective in the sentence. More than one answer may be possible.

EXAMPLE:
Coventry is a modern _____ town.

Coventry is a modern industrial town.

busy	polluted	small
peaceful	sleepy	pretty
old	cosmopolitan	industrial

1 My uncle lives in a _____ picturesque village in Wales.

2 Manchester is a crowded _____ city with lots going on.

3 Avignon is an attractive _____ city with its Papal palace and 14th-century bridge.

4 I'd like to live in a small _____ town with no traffic, noise or pollution.

5 Any industrial city is normally a big _____ place which is difficult to live in.

6 Stratford is a _____ little town in Warwickshire.

page 24   UNIT 3 Stage one

3 Pronunciation

Stress or emphasis is very important when you are speaking English. Key words like adjectives, nouns and verbs are normally stressed. With long words it is important to get the stress right.

Listen to the following words on the tape and mark the stressed syllable in each. The first one has been done for you.

▪lovely   beautiful   surrounded   intense   cathedral

Look at these words and try to do the same. Remember that sometimes we do not pronounce all the syllables in long words.

interest	cultural	crowded
motorway	industry	lively
countryside	excellent	outskirts
polluted	attractive	minutes
located	industrial	restaurants

Now listen to the words on the tape and check your answers.

4 Prepositions
(Language review 1, page 32)

We use prepositions to describe location, distance and motion. Look at the following examples with *in*, *on*, *away* and *by* and say if they refer to location, distance or motion.

1. The airport is 9 miles away.
2. San Francisco is on the west coast of the USA.
3. We're living in the centre of the city.
4. The children go to school by bike.
5. Some people prefer to live in the suburbs.
6. Her office is two blocks away from here.
7. I don't like travelling by plane.
8. Paris is situated on the River Seine.

Looking at these examples, when do you think we use *in* and when do we use *on*?

5 Practice

Look at the table of information about other towns and cities. Using Coventry as an example, make sentences with your partner about each place. Then fill in the information about the town or city where you live. Write a short description using the information you have written.

	Turin	Strasbourg	New Orleans	Your town/city
Type of place	large, industrial	small, historic	picturesque, old	
Population	1,199,000	285,000	1,330,000	
Geographical position	N.W. Italy/River Po	N.E. France/border with Germany	S.E. U.S.A./Gulf Coast	
Nearest airport	16 kms	9 kms	4 kms	
Famous for	cars, castle, university	cathedral, pâté de foie	jazz, food	

UNIT 3 Stage one   page 25

6 Reading

Look at Text 2. How long do you think the family have been in San Francisco?

2

Well Angela. Here we are on the west coast! San Francisco is everything I imagined: lovely views, wonderful old buildings and loads to do and see. Yesterday we drove down to Chinatown which is really fascinating.

We're living in the south-west of the city, right on the outskirts in fact, but we're in a very pretty residential area. Bob unfortunately works right in the centre ('downtown') and has about a 30-minute drive during the rush hour. We've been very lucky and have rented a three-bedroomed house with a big garden. There's a park just round the corner and the kids' school is five blocks away so they can go by bike.

The weather is a bit changeable but we get out of the city at the weekends and go down the coast or into the mountains. The cinema and theatre are excellent and so are the restaurants. So ... when are you coming over to see us?

● **Reading for detail**

Now read the passage again and write suitable questions for the following answers.

EXAMPLES:

Where are the family?
Where is San Francisco?

1 On the west coast.
2 It's got lovely views, beautiful old buildings and loads to do and see.
3 In the south-west, on the outskirts.
4 Residential.
5 In the city centre.
6 By car.
7 About 30 minutes.
8 It's a large three-bedroomed house.
9 It's five blocks away.
10 Into the mountains or down the coast.

7 The definite article
(Language review, 2 page 32)

Look at Text 2 again and underline all the examples of the word *the*. What do most of them have in common? These other examples will help you.

1 The river Danube flows through Vienna.
2 The Atlantic Ocean divides Europe from America.
3 Peking is in the east of China.
4 The Suez Canal is in Egypt.
5 The Andes are in South America.
6 The Sahara Desert is the largest desert in the world.

Now look at the following examples where the definite article is *not* used. Why do you think it isn't used in these cases?

a Coventry is in England.
b San Francisco is everything I imagined.
c Yesterday we drove down to Chinatown.
d Fifth Avenue is a famous street in New York.
e Romania is in south-eastern Europe.
f Birmingham International Airport is nine miles from Coventry.

8 Interview and writing

Using the questions you wrote in Exercise 6 to help you, interview your partner about the area he/she lives in. Find out if they like or dislike the area where they live and why. Try to think of some other questions you would like to ask e.g. about sporting and cultural facilities, shops etc. Note down the answers.

Use the information from your notes to write a short description of your partner's area.

page 26   UNIT 3   Stage one

9 Reading

Read Text 3 and decide what the weather was like during the journey.

3

The train had crossed a peninsula, from Hakodate to Mori. We made a complete circuit of Uchiura Bay where the sun was reflected from the water and snow on the shore. We continued along the coast, staying on the main line; inland there were mountain shelves and the occasional volcano. The train began to turn sharply inland, towards Sapporo. People in hats and warm coats were working beside the track, tying poles together to make a snow fence. We left the shore of what was the western limit of the Pacific; within an hour we were arriving in Sapporo. Mr Watanabe, the consulate driver, met me at the station and offered me a guided tour of the city.

From 'The Great Railway Bazaar' by Paul Theroux

● **Understanding**

Read the text again and decide whether the following statements are true or false. Circle the letter T or F.

1 The writer was travelling in Africa. T/**F**
2 It was starting to get dark. T/**F**
3 They were near the sea. **T**/F
4 Some people were building houses near the track. T/**F**
5 It was very cold. T/**F**
6 A taxi was waiting for the writer at the station. T/**F**

10 Vocabulary

Decide whether the following phrases from Text 3 are matched with the correct diagram. If not, choose the right combination. The example is correct.

EXAMPLE:
1 'from Hakodate to Mori'

A

2 'a complete circuit of Uchiura Bay'
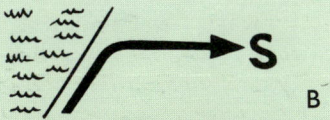
B

3 'The train began to turn sharply inland, towards Sapporo'
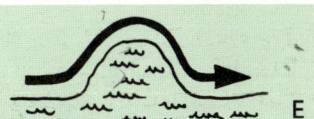
E

4 'We continued along the coast'
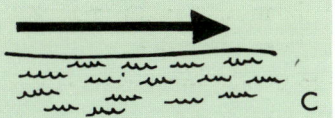
C

5 'People ... were working beside the track'

F

6 'staying on the main line'

D

7 '... we were arriving in Sapporo'
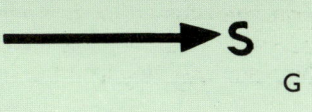
G

Now match the correct diagrams with the following sentences.

1 We had to drive right through the city to find our hotel.
2 There's a post office just round the corner.
3 She stopped in front of the shop.
4 They flew over New York.
5 The man walked under the ladder.
6 He drove past the bank.

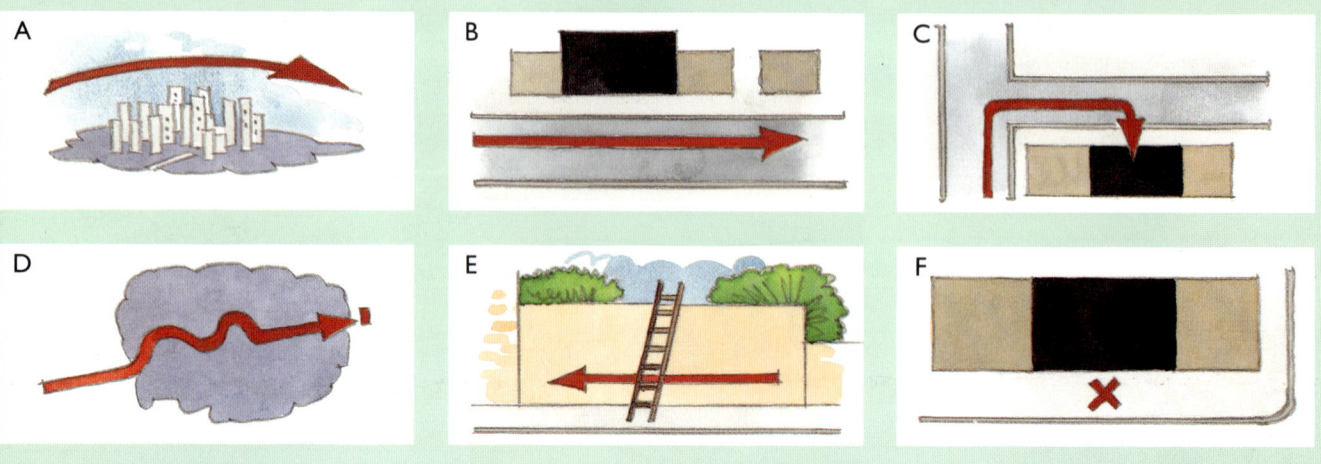

11 Listening

Listen to the conversation in which someone is telling a friend how to get to a place, and answer the questions.

1 Where is Mark going?
2 How is he travelling?
3 How long is it going to take?

Listen to the conversation again and complete Mark's notes.

Now in pairs try to repeat John's instructions from the completed notes, putting in the correct verbs and prepositions. Then draw the route on the map from the town centre to where John lives. Remember that in Britain you drive on the left.

Finally, spend some time planning instructions on how to get to your house and doing a simple map from the nearest station, main road or landmark. Then imagine you are phoning your partner to explain the route. Your partner should draw a map of the route from the instructions and compare it with your original.

page 28   UNIT 3 Stage one

Stage two

Describing Objects

1 Listening

Listen to these people talking about common objects without mentioning their names. Try to guess what the objects are.

Listen again and complete this table.

Object	Material	Shape	Use
1		long, thin handle round head	
2	plastic		
3			wearing at home, relaxing
4		square-shaped	

2 Vocabulary

Take turns with a partner to describe objects in the photograph. Your partner has to guess which object you are describing. Use the words in the boxes to help you.

EXAMPLE: *It's rectangular and it's made of paper.* (newspaper)

SHAPES
round • square • rectangular
oval • long • thin
short • wide

triangular   cylindrical

narrow

MATERIALS
wood • china • paper
glass • cotton • fabric
metal • plastic • wool

UNIT 3 Stage two

3 Describing objects
(Language review 3, page 32)

Look at the descriptions below and put a tick (√) beside the ones that talk about the use or purpose of something.

1 They're made of rubber. ☐
2 It's really easy to use. ☐
3 They're great for relaxing at the end of the day. ☐
4 It's got a plastic base. ☐
5 It switches itself off. ☐
6 This one's very modern. ☐
7 They're for jogging or walking. ☐
8 These are really comfortable. ☐

● Order of adjectives
(Language review 4, page 32)

Look at these examples and try to decide what order adjectives are used in. Think about colour, size, material and shape.

1 He was wearing a new pair of cream leather gloves.
2 What a lovely old wooden chair!
3 I don't like those huge, square, concrete car parks.
4 She had a thin, round gold bracelet on her wrist.
5 That's a horrible, old, fur coat.

Where in the sentence do you think we use adjectives of opinion e.g. *lovely, nice, horrible, beautiful*?

4 Pronunciation

The sounds /ɪ/ and /iː/ are sometimes confused but they are quite different.

EXAMPLE: *this* /ɪ/   *these* /iː/

Listen to and repeat the examples on the tape.

Now in pairs read the dialogue. Underline all the examples of /ɪ/ and /iː/ and put the words into two lists.

(Telephone rings)

Jenny Hello. 21544
Bob Hi Jenny, it's Bob.
Jenny Bob! How are you? I haven't seen you for ages.
Bob No. I've been at a conference in Italy for two weeks.
Jenny Really? That sounds great. Where were you?
Bob Milan. Lovely city. Look Jenny, are you free tomorrow evening?
Jenny Er, it's a bit difficult. I've got to visit my mother.
Bob Oh well, what about later on? We could go to the cinema maybe.
Jenny All right, but give me a ring at work just to confirm it, O.K.?
Bob Yes, I'll phone you around eleven.

Listen to the dialogue to check if your words are correct.

5 Reading and writing

Read this notice. Where would you see something like this?

LOST
A red leather address book with gold letters on the front. It has my name in it and some holiday photos. It's pocket-size and a bit old and torn.
If you find it please contact Laura
(tel. 549243)

Now write a similar notice describing two of your personal possessions.

6 Game

In groups of three take it in turns to describe an object without naming it. The other two people in the group have to try and guess what the object is.

EXAMPLE: *It's normally round and made of wood or glass. It's used for putting fruit in or other kinds of food. You put it in the middle of the table for a meal or just for decoration. What is it?*

page 30 | UNIT 3 Stage two

Activity

Holiday of a Lifetime

1 Reading and understanding

Look at the advertisements for different holidays and match each one with one of the titles. Compare your answers with your partner.

1 Visit the exotic city of Cairo, explore the world-famous pyramids and see the Sphinx, travel through the Valley of the Kings and sail down the Nile to the ancient city of Luxor on the voyage of a lifetime. Unbelievable prices from £598.00 excluding airfare.

2 The towering, snow-capped Rocky Mountains. Hidden lakes. Secret glacier-covered valleys. The scenery of this area is some of the most breathtaking in the world. Here you can walk, climb, camp, canoe or just relax and enjoy the view! Prices from £1250.00 to around £2500.00 including flights.

3 Africa offers unique possibilities for nature-lovers. The Serengeti National Park in Tanzania is teeming with different species of animals. You will also be able to visit Lake Victoria and Mount Kilimanjaro - two of the major attractions in this area. 7 nights holiday. Full board on safari with return flights on British Airways from only £699.00.

4 Around the Canary Islands on a beautiful 35-foot yacht. Away from the tourist traps. One or two weeks from 1st October. No experience needed – skipper will instruct. Would suit outgoing people. £160.00 p.w. plus flight.

- HOLIDAY CANADA – ALBERTA
- COME SAILING IN THE SUN
- WILDLIFE SAFARI
- EGYPT – LAND OF THE PHARAOHS

2 Discussion

In groups of three discuss the type of holiday you would prefer and try to agree on one. You should also say which part of the world the holiday would be in. You will need to consider the following factors:

- The location
- The weather
- Your interests
- The cost
- The type of country

Then make a list for your holiday of things you think you should take with you (e.g. clothing, equipment, documents, medicine).

3 Reading and writing

Read the extract from a letter a friend has written. Then write back telling him/her about the holiday you have just chosen, where you are going, what you will need to take, and the cost. Invite your friend to join you.

Start and end your letter like this:

I've been very busy in the office – I seem to have meetings every day. How about you?

Listen. I've got four weeks holiday this summer and I was wondering if you had any plans. Maybe we could do something together. What do you think? I can take my holiday any time during the summer and I don't really mind where I go or what I do. Anyway, let me know.

Give your parents my best wishes. Hope to hear from you soon.

Best wishes,

```
                                Your address
                                Date
Dear
Thank you for your letter. It was really
nice to hear from you.
```

```
                    Best wishes,
                 (Your first name)
```

UNIT 3 Activity   page 31

Language review

1 Prepositions

● Location

We use *in* for talking about regions or areas of a town or city:

*In the north/south/north-east
in the centre/suburbs*

We use *on* on talk about location on rivers, coasts and limits:

*on the Thames, on the west Atlantic coast,
on the edge of town, on the outskirts*

● Distance

We use *away* to talk about the time or distance to somewhere:

*The airport is nine miles away.
Their school is two blocks away.
Her house is ten minutes away from here.*

● Motion

We use *by* to talk about how we travel:
by bus/car/train/plane/bike

but we say *on foot.*

Notice that *arrive* can be used in three different ways:

You arrive *in* a country, city or town:
*They arrived in Spain last week.
When did you arrive in London?*

You arrive *at* other places or events:
*I always arrive at work late.
What time did he arrive at the meeting?
She's arriving at Heathrow airport.*

You arrive *home* (no preposition):
We arrived home really late last night.

This is the same with any verb of motion:
come, go, leave, drive, walk

2 The definite article

We frequently use *the* when we are talking about location:
the centre, the east, the coast, the outskirts

We also use *the* for the names of rivers, seas, oceans and canals:
the river Seine, the Red Sea, the Pacific Ocean, the Suez Canal

We do not use the definite article in the following cases:
names of continents -
Africa, Asia, South America, Europe

names of countries -
Turkey, Brazil, England, Algeria *

names of towns and cities -
Moscow, Athens, Nairobi; Vancouver

names of streets, roads, avenues, parks and squares -
Regent Street, Kings' Road, Fifth Avenue, Hyde Park, Central Park, Trafalgar Square

Although we say *the east, the west* etc., we do not use *the* for *eastern, western*, etc.:

*Hungary is in eastern Europe.
Marseilles is in southern France.*

* When we talk about the political organisation of a country, we do use *the*:

the United States, the USSR, the United Kingdom, the People's Republic of China

We also use *the* to talk about islands and other plural names:

the Philippines, the Seychelles, the Netherlands

3 Describing objects

● Shape and material

*It's round/square/rectangular,
square-shaped/long/thin.
It's made of wood/glass/plastic.
They're plastic cups/leather shoes.*

● Use/purpose

*I use it for making soups.
It's perfect/great/useless/no good for making tea and coffee.
They're for jogging.
It's to make you relax.*

4 Order of adjectives

Sometimes we use several adjectives to describe something:

He took out a small, round, gold watch.

It is unusual to use a very long list of adjectives but there is a definite order we normally follow for adjectives of fact:

size - shape - colour - material + noun

Opinion adjectives - *nice, horrible, lovely, nasty* etc. - come first:

He took out a beautiful, small, round, gold watch.

UNIT 4
Opener

◆ Complete the words below and match them with the pictures.

a) _a_e_ _k__n_   f) _o_f
b) c_c_i_g   g) h__i_g
c) _n_ok__   h) _is__n_
d) _a_c_i_g _v   i) _h_s_
e) _o_ter_   j) _ra_i_g

◆ What do you do in your spare time? Talk about your favourite and least favourite sport or hobby with a partner.

UNIT 4 Opener   page 33

Stage one

Leisure Activities

1 Listening

Listen to the conversation between a group of friends. Where are they? How many activities do they talk about? What do they finally decide to do?

Listen to the cassette again and decide whether these statements are true or false.

1 The man who arrived late had a Coke.   T/F
2 The weather is very nice.   T/F
3 There are some tennis courts in a park.   T/F
4 They haven't got any equipment to play tennis. T/F
5 Not many people will be swimming.   T/F
6 They need to get some food for the picnic. T/F
7 It's almost 1.50.   T/F
8 One of them doesn't know how to swim.   T/F

2 Vocabulary

1 List each of the sports/activities under one of the three headings. An example of each has been done for you.

swimming	hockey	basketball
gymnastics	climbing	riding
squash	aerobics	billiards
athletics	walking	baseball
exercise	jogging	football
skating	rugby	ballet
judo	chess	darts
sailing	cricket	badminton
volleyball		

| **do** | **play** | **go** |
| *exercise* | *hockey* | *climbing* |

2 What do we call people who do these sports/activities? Write down the names for each one (except *aerobics*, *exercise* and *judo*).

EXAMPLES:

hockey   *hockey player*

athletics   *athlete*

3 Suggestions and opinions
(Language review 1 and 2, page 39)

Look at these phrases from the tapescript and say which are used to
a) make suggestions   b) respond to a suggestion
c) give an opinion.

1 We could have a picnic lunch.
2 Good idea, Clare.
3 Why don't we have a game of tennis?
4 I think we should get some fruit as well.
5 How about hiring a boat?
6 I'm afraid I'm useless at tennis.
7 That sounds great.
8 But it'll be packed with people.

4 Pronunciation

1 You are going to hear ten sentences which contain the ten words below. Listen to each sentence and decide whether the words are pronounced with /ɪə/ or /ɛə/. Put the words into the correct column. The first two have been done for you.

1 clear	6 beer
2 their	7 disappear
3 fairly	8 there
4 near	9 here
5 chair	10 hair

| /ɪə/ | /ɛə/ |
| clear | their |

page 34   UNIT 4   Stage one

2 Read these sentences in pairs and decide whether the words in italics are pronounced with /ɪə/ or /ɛə/.

1 *Where's* the soap?
2 *Careful* or you'll *tear* the paper.
3 Jane *shares* a flat with two other people.
4 *Fear* of flying is very common.
5 I need a new *pair* of shoes.
6 I can't *hear* what he's saying.

5 Practice

Look at the following information and in groups of three decide how you would like to spend an evening in Oxford, including dinner at a restaurant. When you have finished, report to the other groups what you have chosen and the reasons for your choices. Make suggestions and give responses or preferences.

EXAMPLE: *Let's go and listen to some jazz.*
I'm not very keen on jazz. I'd prefer to go to the theatre.

OXFORD INFORMATION SHEET

CINEMAS
Phoenix 1
'Batman' 4.30 p.m., 6.45 p.m., 9.00 p.m.
Phoenix 2
'When Harry Met Sally' 3.45 p.m., 7.15 p.m., 8.30 p.m.
A.B.C.
'The Last Emperor' 3.00 p.m., 5.15 p.m., 7.30 p.m.

THEATRES
New Theatre
Welsh National Opera in 'Cosi Fan Tutti', Mozart 3.00 p.m., 7.00 p.m.
Playhouse
English Shakespeare Comany in 'Romeo & Juliet'

LIVE MUSIC
The Brewhouse
Jazz every night from 8.30 p.m.
The New Inn
Rock 'n Roll Thurs-Sat from 8.00 p.m.
The Anchor
Folk music Wed & Fri 8.30 p.m. onwards.

DISCOS
Tramps
The best of pop music plus light show 9.00 p.m. - 3.00 a.m.
Bogart's
Music for every taste – salsa, rock, heavy metal 10.30 p.m. - 3.30 a.m.

RESTAURANTS
The Moonlight Indian Restaurant. Delicious Indian food at reasonable prices. 46 Cowley Road.
The Opium Den. The best Chinese restaurant in town. Specialising in Cantonese Food. Fully licensed. 3 New Road.
Pizzaland. The biggest range of pizzas anywhere! Happy Hour 5.00-6.00 p.m. 12 High Street.
MacDonald's. The last word in hamburgers at an unbeatable price. 6 Cornmarket.

CONCERTS
The Sheldonian Theatre
The English Chamber Orchestra play music by Bach and Handel, Thurs-Sat 7.30 p.m.
Clarendon Rooms
New College Choir sing religious music by Brahms and Purcell.

Information valid until 28th July

Stage two

Favourite Things

1 Reading

Read the following extract. Where do you think the passage comes from? What kind of person is being interviewed? What kind of language is being used?

Garlic bread ... Garlic bread is my absolute favourite food, and I eat loads of it. It doesn't matter at all that it gives me bad breath, I just love it so much. I don't pretend to be the greatest chef in the world, but I do enjoy cooking. When I have time I like to try and prepare something exotic like Japanese food. I'll eat just about anything that's put in front of me as long as it's cooked well, and isn't Brussels sprouts – I hate Brussels sprouts more than anything in the world.

Music ... My favourite song? That's a tough one. I just bought 'Love Changes Everything' so I guess that's one of my favourites at the moment. I was really into the Beatles as a young kid. There isn't much music I don't like ... I'm not particularly into opera, in fact I can't stand opera. I just don't take to it.

New York, London and Maui ... My favourite place in the world is, I guess, a place called Maui in Hawaii. Ooh actually there's two places, Maui and New York, oh, and London – that's three now. I like all those because they're so different from home. Also I love getting in the car and going for a drive down to the beach. Yeah, the beach is one of my favourite places too.

Clothes ... I'm most at home wearing casual clothes like jeans and T-shirts and black shoes. I do like dressing up for special occasions but I'm not very keen on wearing suits and ties.

Heroes ... One of my favourites in the acting profession at the moment is Michael Douglas. I think he's a brilliant actor. I'd love to be in a film like *Fatal Attraction* or *Wall Street* with him.

TV programme ... There's a show in Australia called *The Comedy Company* and it's really funny, so that would be one of my favourite shows. I hardly watch TV at all, and to be honest I don't like TV that much.

From an interview with Jason Donovan in 'Just 17' magazine

● **Understanding**

Read this summary introducing Jason Donovan and make any necessary corrections by checking with the text you have just read.

Jason Donovan is an Australian actor and pop singer. He first became famous in the T.V. series *Neighbours*. He's not very fond of cooking but really likes garlic bread and brussel sprouts. He hates opera but he was very keen on the Beatles when he was younger. Now he prefers walking to driving a car. He has two favourite cities: Maui and New York. He prefers smart clothes and is very keen on dressing up for a special night out and loves wearing suits. He likes comedy programmes but in general dislikes TV.

page 36   UNIT 4 Stage two

2 Vocabulary

We can talk about categories of words. For example, *sofa, chair, table* and *bed* can be classified under *furniture*. In other words they are examples of this category.

Look at the following groups of words (some of them are from the text) and decide on suitable categories.

Examples	Category
Brussels sprouts, bread, apples	
jeans, T-shirt, suit	
opera, jazz, rock	
surfing, swimming, tennis	
chess, darts, billiards	
orange juice, beer, rum	
'Fatal Attraction', 'Who Framed Roger Rabbit?'	
The Beatles, U2, Dire Straits	
Madonna, Rick Astley, Luciano Pavarotti	

3 Likes and dislikes
(Language review 3, page 39)

In pairs, look at the text again and list in the two columns all the phrases which express likes and dislikes. Two examples have been done for you.

Try to put the phrases in each column in order of stronger to weaker words by numbering them.

LIKES

I love garlic bread.

DISLIKES

I hate Brussels sprouts.

4 Pronunciation

Homophones are words which have the same pronunciation but different meanings. Listen to these two sentences and identify the two words which are homophones.

Look at this list of homophones. Then listen to six more sentences and identify which homophone is being mentioned in each.

1 bean/been
2 flour/flower
3 peace/piece
4 pair/pear
5 sail/sale
6 pour/poor

Finally, can you think of homophones for the following words?

a) groan _____
b) heal _____
c) mail _____
d) son _____
e) stair _____
f) plain _____
g) won _____
h) weather _____

5 Practice

Using the categories you wrote down in Exercise 2, interview your partner, finding out what he/she likes and dislikes in each category.

EXAMPLE: *What kind of food do you like?*

Now collect all the results to produce a survey of opinions in your class.

6 Writing

Using the results from the survey, write a short paragraph about what the people in your class like and dislike and why.

Activity

A Day in the Lake District

1 Reading

The Lake District is in north-west England. In pairs, read the advertisement for activity holidays and mark each of the activities mentioned in the correct place on the map opposite. Use these abbreviations:

W – walking   Cl – climbing   R – riding   G – golf
S – sailing   Ca – canoeing   F – fishing

In the same way, place each event on the map using its number.

Activities in the Lake District

Choose from climbing in the Borrowdale area, riding in Eskdale Green, golf in Ambleside and Bowness, sailing in Coniston and Keswick or fishing in Ravenglass and Ulverston.

The Lake District National Park is of course ideal for a walking holiday, and organised walks with a guide are available in many centres, including Windermere and Newby Bridge.

As you would expect in an area full of beautiful lakes, there are many water-based holidays and you can hire boats on many of the lakes.

If you are one of those people who find just sitting in the sun too boring to contemplate for the whole of your holiday, there is a wide range of Lakeland activity holidays to interest everyone, many offering instruction for complete beginners.

Local Events

1. **May 13–21** Keswick Jazz Festival in the Brewery Arts Centre. Tel: Keswick 2513
2. **June 6–9** Lakeland Flower Show in Windermere Civic Centre. Tel: Windermere 436
3. **July 2–16** Lake Artists' Annual Exhibition staged in Grasmere by the Lake Artists' Society, featuring mainly professional artists resident in Cumbria. Tel: Grasmere 280
4. **August 3–4** Cockermouth Show. A typical Cumbrian agricultural show with livestock, produce and crafts. Tel: Maryport 812925
5. **September 28 & 29** Cartmel Horse Races. The race-course is situated in beautiful parkland outside the attractive little village of Cartmel with its famous 12th century monastery. Tel: Witherslack 228

2 Planning a day trip

In groups of three, plan a day out in the Lake District. Make sure you each say what you like or dislike doing. Also take into account the distances and how long you want to spend doing each activity. Make notes of who wants to do which activity and what you finally decide to do.

3 Listening

Before you start your day you decide to listen to the local radio news. Listen to the recording and make any changes you think necessary in your original plan of activities.

4 Discussion

When you have made any changes to your programme, one member of the group should go to another group to compare the different plans that have been made for the day.

5 Writing

One of your friends is arriving after you leave on your trip. Write a note explaining what you have decided to do and why. Also mention approximately when you will be in each place.

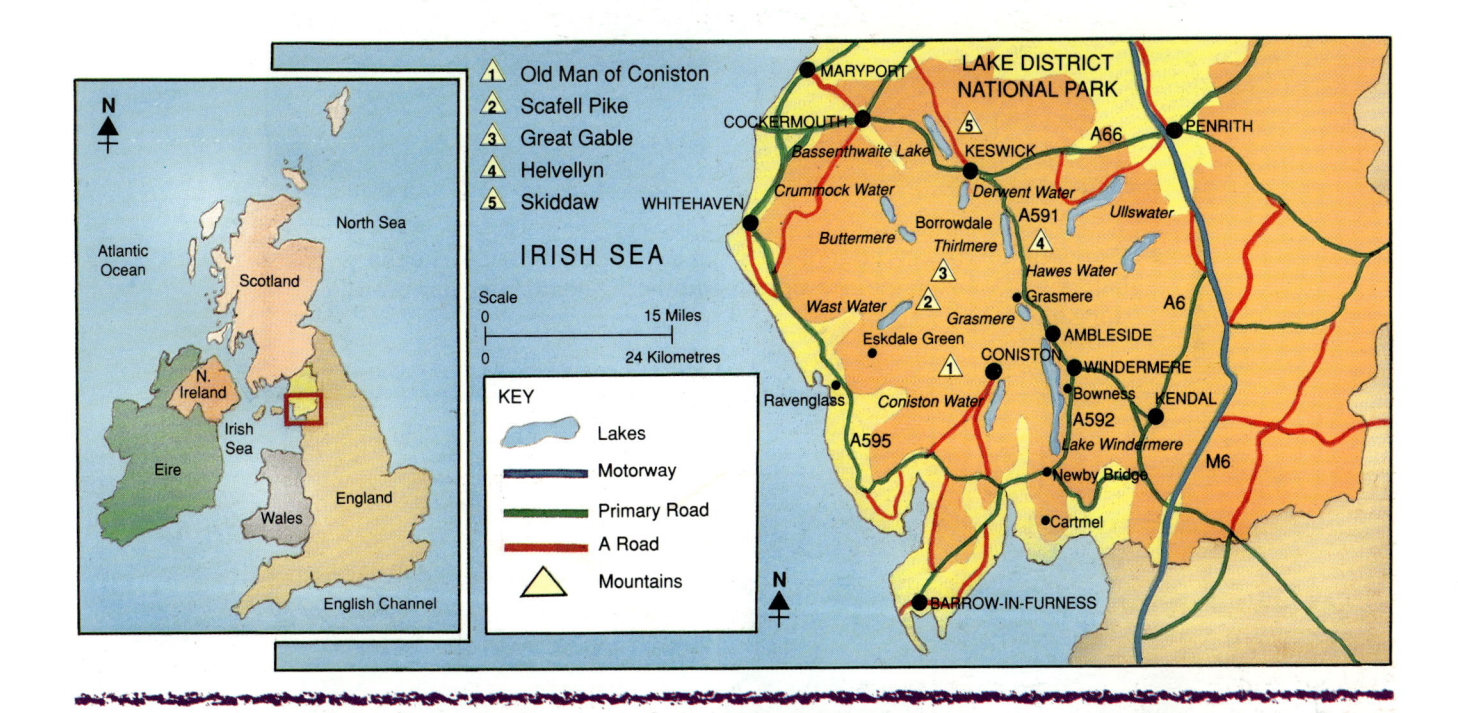

Language review

1 Making suggestions

The following ways of making suggestions are used in this unit.

a) Using a question:

Why don't we have a game of tennis?
How about hiring a boat on the river?
What about having a Chinese meal?

b) Using *let's* or *could*:

Let's go before it gets too late.
We could have a picnic lunch.

2 Responding to suggestions

Notice these different ways of responding to a suggestion:

Why don't we go to the theatre?

POSITIVE RESPONSES	NEGATIVE RESPONSES
Good idea.	Well, it's a bit expensive.
O.K.	But we're too late.
That sounds great!	I'm afraid I don't like the theatre.
That's a nice idea.	Um, how about seeing a film instead?

Expressing preferences/opinions

I'd prefer to go swimming.
I'd (much) rather do something else.
I think we should go skating.

3 Expressing likes and dislikes

Here are some of the verbs which express likes and dislikes:

*like, love, enjoy, be keen on
don't like, hate, can't stand*

These verbs can all be followed either by nouns or by *-ing* form verbs:

NOUNS	-ING FORMS
I don't like chocolate.	I love watching films
He quite likes jazz.	I'm not keen on singing.
I can't stand Monday mornings.	Do you like going to the theatre?
Do you enjoy your work?	The kids really like playing Nintendo.

UNIT 5

Opener

◆ Work out the correct order of events in this cartoon story. Write the letters A - G next to the appropriate number. (The first one has been done for you.)

1 _D_   5 _____

2 _____   6 _____

3 _____   7 _____

4 _____

◆ Compare your order of events with your partner's.

◆ Car Boot Sales are very popular in Britain. What do you think they are?

page 40   UNIT 5 Opener

Stage one

Relating Experiences

1 Reading

Read quickly through this jumbled newspaper story and guess which word has been replaced by ***

Read the story again and put the eleven parts (A - K) into the correct order.

Leeds newsboy earns praise for quick action

A He saw lots of wires and a battery, and he knew straight away that there was a *** in it.

B As soon as they discovered this, soldiers blocked off the street and experts destroyed the *** with a controlled explosion.

C They only believed him when they saw the story on TV later.

D Yesterday, West Yorkshire Police praised 15-year-old Andrew Webster of Leeds for the way he reacted to a *** he found on his early-morning paper round recently.

E Immediately after Andrew's call, the police contacted an Army *** disposal team, who found that it was a sophisticated fire ***, with a special mechanism to make it go off if anyone tried to move it.

F Afterwards, Army scientists took the remains away for examination.

G Then he left the phone booth and delivered the rest of his newspapers.

H Andrew spotted a woman's handbag in a telephone kiosk near the newsagents he worked for in Roundhay Road, Leeds.

I Finally, when he got to school, Andrew told all his friends about the ***. Of course, they laughed at him.

J Next he dialled 999 from the same call box and told the police about the ***. They said they'd come and investigate immediately.

K First of all, he went in to look for an address so that he could return it to the owner, but he got a shock when he looked inside the bag.

Local hero, Andrew Webster

● Understanding

Find or work out the answers to these questions.

1 Why did Andrew look inside the handbag?
2 Why do you think Andrew telephoned the police from the same call box?
3 Why do you think the soldiers blocked off the street?
4 Why do you think the Army wanted to examine the remains?
5 Why do you think Andrew's friends didn't believe his story at first?
6 Why did they change their minds?

2 Reference

What do the words in *italics* in these extracts from the text refer to?

1 ... a bomb in *it*.   (Extract A)
2 ... they discovered *this* ...   (B)
3 *They* only believed *him* ...   (C)
4 ... *it* was a sophisticated fire bomb ...   (E)
5 ... *they* laughed at *him*.   (I)
6 *They* said they'd come ...   (J)
7 ... return *it* to the owner ...   (K)

UNIT 5 Stage one   page 41

3 Vocabulary

● Telephones

1 Find three phrases in the text which mean 'a public place where people can make telephone calls'.

2 Complete these three sentences with appropriate verbs in the Past Simple. The sentences all mean the same as: 'Andrew contacted the police using the telephone.'

a Andrew _____ the police.

b Andrew _____ the police up.

c Andrew made a _____ _____ to the police.

● Meanings

Match these verbs from the text with their meanings.

1	to praise	a	to have an (unpleasant) surprise
2	to spot	b	to say nice things about
3	to return	c	to examine or look into carefully
4	to get a shock	d	to accept that something (someone says) is true
5	to investigate	e	to take, give or send back
6	to destroy	f	to notice, to see
7	to believe	g	to ruin completely, to make useless

4 Sequences of events
(Language review 1, page 49)

Which words or phrases in the text in Exercise 1 tell you ...

1 ... that Andrew went to look inside the bag before he did anything else? _____

2 ... that Andrew telephoned the police after he saw the bomb? _____

3 ... that Andrew delivered the rest of his newspapers after he phoned the police? _____

4 ... that the last thing that Andrew did that morning was to go to school? _____

5 ... when the police called in the bomb disposal men. _____

6 ... when the soldiers blocked off the street. _____

7 ... that the last thing the Army did was to take away the remains of the bomb. _____

5 Story-telling

Working in pairs, make up a story called *'The Day Everything Went Wrong'*.

Use as many of the words and phrases in this box as you can in your story.

> first of all • then • next • afterwards • finally
> as soon as • (immediately) after

You and your partner should make up alternate lines of the story.

EXAMPLE:

Student A   *It was a terrible day. First I got up late and had no time for breakfast.*

Student B   *Then I had a car accident on the way to work. I broke my arm and had to go to hospital.*

Student A   ...

Tell your story to another pair of students.

6 Listening

Listen to this radio interview with Andrew Webster. How late for school was Andrew?

Now listen again and make a list of the differences between the newspaper story on page 41 and the story Andrew tells the interviewer.

7 Pronunciation

Listen to the cassette and repeat the six questions from the interview.

Does the interviewer's voice rise (go up) or fall (go down) at the end of the questions?

Listen again and write R or F for each sentence. (The first one has been done for you.)

1 _R_   2 _____   3 _____
4 _____   5 _____   6 _____

Which questions rise and which questions fall? Compare ideas with a partner.

8 Punchlines

Work in groups of four.

You are going to make up short stories. Student A starts the story, Student B makes up the second sentence, Student C the third, etc.

Each of you should secretly choose one of these five punchlines. You have to try to end the story with your punchline.

1 *Finally he went to sleep with it still in his mouth.*

2 *Afterwards we picked them up, washed them, and ate them.*

3 *As soon as it arrived, we cut all its legs off.*

4 *Finally he took it out of his pocket and threw it at his brother.*

5 *After that we couldn't move for nearly three days.*

The winner is the student who finishes the story with his/her punchline, in a way which makes sense.

9 Talking about experiences
(Language review 2, page 49)

1 The interviewer asks Andrew this question:

Have you ever been on the radio before?

This is a question about Andrew's past experience.

From memory, write Andrew's answer and then check by looking at the tapescript on page 147. Look for more examples of this verb tense in the script.

2 What is the difference between Type A and Type B sentences? Compare your ideas with a partner.

Type A I've flown from London to New York.
He's worked abroad.
I've met the President three times.
We've been to Russia.

Type B I flew from London to New York last week.
He worked abroad from 1987 to 1990.
I met the President in December.
Last year we went to Russia.

10 Have you ever ...?

Write two lists:

1 Things I'd like to do.
   EXAMPLE: *I'd like to visit the United States.*

2 Unpleasant things that happened to you recently.
   EXAMPLE: *I broke my leg.*

Try to find someone in your class who has done these things. Ask questions like this:

Have you ever visited America?
Have you ever broken your leg?

UNIT 5 Stage one

Stage two

Dramatic Events

1 Pairwork

Choose one of these storm scenes and describe what you think happened before the photograph was taken.

Compare your ideas with another pair of students.

2 Listening

Listen to this husband and wife remembering the night of October 15/16th 1987 in England. Who do you think got out of bed first on the night of the storm – the man or the woman? How do you know?

3 Making questions

Listen to the cassette again and make up suitable questions for these answers.

EXAMPLE:

Question *Why couldn't the woman move?*

Answer Because her legs were trapped by a wooden beam.

1 **Question** _____ ?

   Answer Because she wanted to protect herself.

2 **Question** _____ ?

   Answer Because she heard it miaowing.

3 **Question** _____ ?

   Answer Because he wanted to check that the children were all right.

4 **Question** _____ ?

   Answer Because she was terrified by the noise of the storm.

5 **Question** _____ ?

   Answer Because he could hear her crying.

4 Listening

What were Becky, Laura, Matthew and Tom doing when their father came into their rooms? Listen to the Exercise 2 recording again and make notes.

Now listen to the children talking. As you listen, work out who is speaking in each case.

page 44   UNIT 5 Stage two

● **Understanding**

Match these sentence beginnings with their correct endings.

1 It was still dark, so …
2 She was only half awake, so …
3 Laura decided to get dressed …
4 When Tom opened his curtains, …
5 Before Tom heard his mother scream, …
6 When his father burst in, …
7 Becky thought there was a war …
8 Becky hid under Laura's bed because …

a … Matthew saw the trees swaying.
b … Tom was watching the storm.
c … he heard his father shout.
d … she had no idea what was happening.
e … because of the awful noise.
f … and go downstairs.
g … she was terrified.
h … Laura knew it wasn't morning.

5 Sequence words

Listen to the children again. Tick which of these sequence words and phrases you hear.

after than ☐   as soon as ☐
first of all ☐   first ☑
in the end ☑   the next thing I remember ☐
then ☐   the next thing I knew ☑

6 Adjectives: -ing or -ed?

1 Look at these two sentences:

The storm was **terrifying**.
I was **terrified**.

What is the difference in meaning between the words *terrifying* and *terrified*? Compare ideas with a partner.

2 Choose the correct form of the adjective in these sentences:

a The concert was so *boring/bored* that we left at the interval.
b We were really *surprising/surprised* to hear your news.
c The storm was a *frightening/frightened* experience for animals.
d We listened to every word he said – he was such an *interesting/interested* speaker.
e I haven't heard from my sister for nearly a year. I'm quite *worrying/worried* about her.

7 Hearing and seeing
(Language review 3, page 49)

1 Read these sentences:

I **heard** the cat **miaowing**.
I **saw** my youngest son **staring** out of the window.

Now read these sentences:

Next, I **heard** Dad **shout**.
I **saw** the tree **crash** to the ground.

Why are the verbs *see* and *hear* sometimes followed by the *-ing* form and sometimes by the infinitive? Compare ideas with a partner.

2 Look at the three storm photographs again. Imagine yourself in one of these situations:

Photo 1: You were driving home from a party in this car.
Photo 2: You were asleep in a bedroom in the house.
Photo 3: You were taking your dog for a walk in the woods.

Describe what you saw and heard.

8 Talking about past events
(Language review 1 and 4, page 49)

Question What was happening when the woman woke up?
Answer The roof **was falling in** around her.

Make up some more answers like this to describe what was happening (the situation) when the woman woke up. Use your imagination.

UNIT 5 Stage two   page **45**

Question What did the man do when he woke up?

Answer He **leapt** out of bed.

Make up some more answers like this to describe what the man did next. Use your imagination or refer to the tapescript on page 148.

9 Reading and practice

Read about these people's worst journeys.

Homework

Travelling luggage

Bruce Oldfield, one of Britain's top fashion designers, is used to bad luck when travelling. "Just last month I was on a plane from Denver to Aspen and the engine caught fire. It was terrible. I was travelling with a load of models who all started screaming. It was actually very frightening. But we managed to land and everything was handled very professionally and safely."

But his worst journey was when he was trying to fly to the Dominican Republic for Christmas and was held up for more than ten hours. "Everyone had to remain together with their luggage. It was basically me and 150 Dominicans who, for some reason, were all taking fridges and cookers and other electrical goods home. What a holiday that was."

Strange encounter

It was pitch dark when Derek Nimmo arrived at Tehran airport. He knew nobody and had no hotel booked. To make matters worse, the Shah of Iran was celebrating 2,000 years of monarchy in his country and almost every westernised hotel was full.

"I just didn't know where to go. So after a lot of asking I had to trust my luck with a taxi driver to whom I explained that any hotel would do as long as it had a bed," remembers the actor and comedian.

"He took me to a very sleazy-looking hotel and everything was fine until about 3am. Then a strange man came into my room, took off all his clothes and got into the bed next to mine. I went back to sleep and when I woke I found he had gone."

page 46 UNIT 5 Stage two

Snail's pace

For Michael Checkland, the Director General of the BBC, his worst travelling experience was six years ago, driving from Birmingham to London in a terrible snowstorm.

Michael had four children in his car as he fought his way through the terrible blizzard at a snail's pace. Instead of taking an hour and a half he was on the road for more than six.

"It really was quite frightening. One of the children had to walk in front of the car to see if there was anything in front because visibility was so bad. We kept having to take diversions as roads were closed and at times we had the feeling that we were never going to get home. We had to crawl at a terribly slow pace at times because we just couldn't see what was a couple of yards ahead."

Make notes in a table like this:

Now write about your own worst journey. Describe the situation and say what happened.

Find out about your partner's worst journey by asking questions. Your partner can answer only *Yes* or *No*.

EXAMPLE: **A** *Were you travelling by car?*
  B *No, I wasn't.*
  A *Were you walking?*
  B *…*

	Situation	Events
Bruce Oldfield	1 He was flying from Denver to Aspen. 2	
Derek Nimmo		He caught a taxi. The taxi took him to a cheap hotel.
Michael Checkland		

---

*A*ctivity

Road Accident

1 Listening

Listen to this radio report of a road accident. How was the driver of the Sierra injured?

Listen again and make notes under these headings:

Location of accident _____

Time _____

Number of people involved _____

Vehicles involved _____

Police telephone number _____

2 Discussion

How do you think the accident happened? Look at this police diagram of the scene of the accident, and listen to the radio report again if necessary.

Compare ideas with a partner.

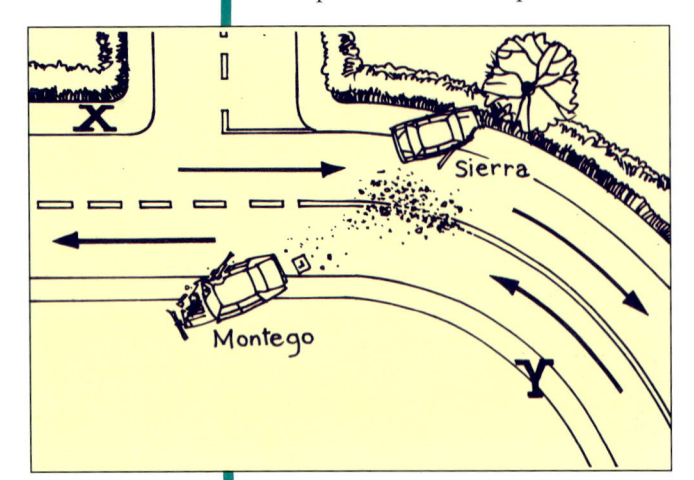

3 Writing and reporting back

Work in groups of four.

Write a short account of how the accident happened. Describe the situation and conditions before the accident, and then relate the sequence of events.

Student A You were the driver of the Montego.

Student B You were the passenger in the Sierra.

Student C You were a witness to the accident. You were standing at the point marked **X** on the map when the accident occurred.

Student D You were a witness to the accident. You were standing at the point marked **Y** on the map when the accident occurred.

Take turns to tell the rest of your group how you think the accident happened.

Discuss which is the most probable description of the accident.

4 Reading

Turn to page 142 and read the police description of what actually happened. Whose description of the accident is the most accurate?

5 Writing

Write a short letter describing an accident you were involved in personally. Write about any kind of accident.

EXAMPLES: • on the road   • at home   • at work
• at school/college   • while doing sport

Set the scene for your story with a description of the situation and the people involved.

Describe the sequence of events. (What happened first? Then what? And next?) Don't finish the story.

Exchange stories with a partner. Read your partner's story and try to guess the ending.

UNIT 5 Activity

Language review

1 Sequencers

We use these words and phrases to refer to the order or sequence of actions or events:

1 first   firstly   first of all   to start with
2 then   next   afterwards   later   after that
3 finally   in the end

EXAMPLES:

First of all he went in to look for an address.
Then he telephoned the police.
Finally he went to school.

We use these words and phrases to link two actions or events:

as soon as   when   after   before

EXAMPLES:

As soon as they discovered this, the soldiers blocked off the street.
When everything was over, I went home.
After he looked in the bag, Andrew phoned the police.
The army blocked off the street before they destroyed the bomb.

We also use *before* and *after* as prepositions:

Before school, Andrew delivers papers.
After Andrew's call, the police contacted the Army.

2 The Present Perfect Simple

● **Form**

have/has + past participle. Examples:

I've done my homework.
He has never been to London.

In this unit the Present Perfect Simple is used to refer to people's past experiences:

Interviewer: *Have you ever been on the radio before?*
  Andrew: *No, I haven't.*
Interviewer: *Have you ever see a bomb before?*
  Andrew: *I've only seen them on the telly.*

We use the Present Perfect when we are looking back at the past from the present:

I've never seen a bomb. (until today)
I've just finished my lunch. (I'm not hungry now.)
I've already seen that film. (I don't want to see it again today.)
She hasn't written yet. (I expected a letter before now.)
Have you ever been to London? (before today)

When we want to say exactly when something happened, we use the Past Simple, not the Present Perfect:

Q: *Have you seen that film yet?*
A: *Yes, I saw it yesterday.*
Q: *Has he ever been to London?*
A: *Yes, he went there last week.*

3 Hear and see

The verbs *hear* and *see* can be followed by the infinitive or the *-ing* form.

We use the infinitive when we heard or saw a **complete** action from before it began until it ended:

I heard Dad **shout**.
I saw the tree **fall**.

We use the *-ing* form when we saw or heard only a **part** of the action:

I heard the cat **miaowing**.
I saw Tom staring *out of the* **window**.

The verb *feel* can be used in the same way:

I felt the insect **crawl/crawling** *across my hand.*

Verbs of perception (e.g. *see, hear, feel*) are often used with *can/could*:

I **can hear** *the cat miaowing.*
I **could feel** *the insect crawl across my hand.*

4 The Past Continuous

● **Form**

was/were + *-ing* form:

I was reading the newspaper.
They were working all evening.

In this unit the Past Continuous is used to refer to an event or action that was in progress in the past:

Matthew was sleeping peacefully.
Becky was hiding under the bed.

If two actions were in progress at the same time, *while* can be used to link them:

While *Matthew was sleeping peacefully, Becky was hiding under the bed.*

The Past Continuous can be used with the Past Simple to relate an action in progress to a single event:

When I woke up, the roof was falling around me.
I was standing watching the storm when Dad burst in.

UNIT 5 Language review   page 49

UNIT 6

Opener

◆ Look at these different products.

1 What connection is there between them?
2 Do you buy any of these kinds of things?

◆ Discuss these points with a partner.

1 What health issue or danger is each product concerned with?
2 How seriously do you take these dangers? Put them into an order of seriousness. (1 = very serious; 10 = not serious at all).
3 Do you worry about your health? Compare worries with your partner.

Stage one

Whose Health Is It Anyway?

1 Listening

Listen to four unfinished conversations.

Which of these health issues are mentioned by the speakers? Put the numbers in four of the boxes.

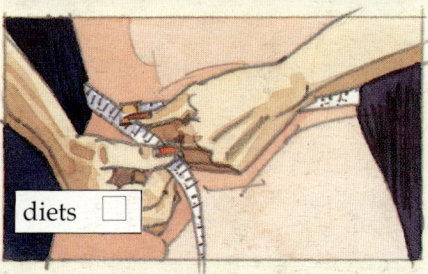

alcohol ☐   fatty food [1]   smoking [2]

exercise [3]   sunbathing [4]   diets ☐

2 Predicting

The four conversations were unfinished.

Listen again and predict what the speakers were going to say next. Here are the four unfinished endings:

1 *It seems to me it's impossible for us to …*
2 *And anyway I don't smoke when …*
3 *Well, I sometimes play …*
4 *They say if you get too much sun …*

P144

3 Vocabulary

● **Classifying words**

Make lists of words under these headings.

Dairy foods	Diseases	Types of exercise
butter	cancer	jogging

● **Definitions**

Some words have more than one meaning. Here are some definitions of words from the four conversations.

Fill the gaps with words from the box and match each word with its correct meaning. (The first one has been done for you.)

campaign • chemical • colouring • dangerous
exercise • expert • fat • fuss • jogging
passive • report • sunbathing

1 **campaign** A a number of connected army actions
              (B) a number of connected activities

2 _____ A colour of a person's skin; complexion
              B substance used to give a particular colour to something (especially food)

3 _____ A a story of something seen or heard
              B a loud noise, a bang (like a gun)

4 _____ A not taking part; inactive
              B the grammatical opposite of active (verbs)

5 _____ A a physical activity, like running
              B knocking something gently

6 _____ A using your body to become healthier or stronger
              B a task, sometimes in a book, to train your brain

UNIT 6 Stage one   page 51

4 Everybody and nobody
(Language review 4, page 58)

The speakers use these two phrases in the conversations:

Nobody really knows what causes cancer.
(This is a mystery.)
But everybody knows that sunbathing is bad for you.
(This is a well-known fact.)

Work in pairs. Think of three more health mysteries and three more well-known health facts. Make sentences starting:

Nobody really knows ... and *Everybody knows ...*

Compare ideas with another pair of students.

---

5 Pronunciation

The most common vowel sound in English speech is the schwa /ə/. This sound occurs in the weak form of many common short words. Look at these examples.

	Strong	Weak
a	eɪ	ə
an	æn	ən
and	ænd	ənd
at	æt	ət
but	bʌt	bət
can	kæn	kən
for	fɔ	fə
had	hæd	həd
have	hæv	həv
that	ðæt	ðət
the	ði	ðə
was	wɒz	wəz

Listen to these sentences from the conversations you heard in Exercise 1.

Are the underlined words strong or weak? Write S or W above each word. (The first sentence has been done for you.)

1 <u>A</u> few years ago they <u>had</u> <u>a</u> campaign against butter.   (W S W)
2 They said it <u>was</u> bad <u>for</u> your heart.
3 <u>Have</u> you heard <u>the</u> latest report about smoking?
4 If you live or work with smokers you <u>can</u> get cancer <u>and</u> heart disease.
5 You're only saying <u>that</u> because you smoke.
6 Do you want <u>to</u> come jogging <u>at</u> <u>the</u> weekend?
7 <u>But</u> everybody knows <u>that</u> sunbathing's bad <u>for</u> you.
8 How <u>can</u> they?
9 I'm not <u>an</u> expert.

---

6 Asking for and giving opinions
(Language review 1, page 58)

Which five of these questions ask someone for their opinions? (Tick the boxes.)

1 Do you want coffee or tea? ☐
2 What's your opinion about colourings in food? ☐
3 What about running in the marathon this year? ☐
4 What do the experts say? ☐
5 What are your views on the problem of stress in modern life? ☐
6 What do you think about the latest health scares? ☐
7 Have you stopped smoking yet? ☐
8 How do you feel about people who drink and drive? ☐
9 I don't think much of the government's policies on drugs, do you? ☐
10 What did your doctor advise you to do? ☐

Now match the opinions with the five questions you have just ticked.

A In my opinion it's a crime. Hundreds of people a year die because of it.

B I think they should be banned completely.

C I believe people work too hard and don't have enough time to relax.

D No, I don't. If you ask me, they should make strict new laws.

E As far as I'm concerned, the so-called experts are talking a lot of nonsense.

7 You, us (we) and they
(Language review 3, page 58)

Notice the uses of *they, you* and *us* in these extracts from Exercise 1.

'Apparently, if *you* live or work with smokers *you* can get cancer …'

'It seems to me it's impossible for *us* to …'

'A few years ago *they* had a campaign against butter. *They* said it was bad for your heart.'

'In my opinion, *they're* making a lot of fuss about nothing.'

'But *they* say if you get too much sun …'

Who do you think *they, you* and *us* are? Compare ideas with a partner.

Now discuss these questions with a partner:

1 What are they doing to make your town a better place to live in?
2 When you're driving a car, how can you avoid having an accident?

8 Reading

What happened to Jennifer Hall on the school bus? Read this text to find out.

Suffering from the school bus smokers

A 13-year-old girl has stayed away from school since Christmas - because under-age smokers on the school bus gave her chronic smokers' cough.

Jennifer Hall was a promising runner and soccer player until she was forced to breathe in cigarette fumes during the twice-daily 45-minute trip from her home in Frieth, Buckinghamshire, to Great Marlow Comprehensive School. Jennifer has no alternative to the bus because she lives more than five miles from the school.

The family's GP confirmed Jennifer is suffering from smoker's cough.

Jennifer said: 'I really hate smoking and would never do it myself, but the school bus is always filled with smoke.

"Now I have this terrible cough and I get really bad headaches. I have been off school since Christmas because I'm too ill to go and my dad won't let me travel on the bus in case all the smoke makes it worse again.

Note: GP = General Practitioner, a non-specialist (family) doctor

What would you do in Jennifer's position? Discuss your ideas with a partner.

9 Vocabulary

Which word or phrase in the text tells you …

1 Jennifer's age?
2 that the school bus smokers are not old enough to smoke?
3 that Jennifer was going to be very good at running and football?
4 how often Jennifer has to make the bus journey between home and school?
5 that Jennifer has no other way of getting to school than by bus?
6 that the last time Jennifer went to school was before Christmas?

10 Discussion

How would you define the phrase 'passive smoking'? Compare definitions with a partner.

Now read this extract from a leaflet about the dangers of passive smoking. Is your definition correct?

> Only 1 out of every 3 people in the UK smokes cigarettes. This means that there are twice as many non-smokers as smokers.
> Breathing in air which contains other people's smoke is called *passive smoking*.
> Until the late 1970s, scientists thought that passive smoking was no more than a nuisance to most non-smokers. But research now shows that it's more than just a nuisance. It can also be a health hazard.

● **Talking points**

1 What can smokers do to reduce the effects of their smoke on other people?
2 What can non-smokers do?

Discuss your ideas with your partner. Try to agree on three different answers to each question.

11 Writing

Here are some questions which young people have asked about smoking. Choose one question and write a letter giving your advice to the questioner.

- Why are so many people against smoking?
- I'd like to try it just once. Surely that isn't a problem, is it?
- My friends smoke. I don't want to start. What should I say to them?
- I play a lot of sport. Will smoking make any difference?

Stage two

Food Facts

1 Pre-reading

You are spending the day in town. You feel hungry and thirsty, but you haven't got much time and you don't want to spend too much money. In this situation what would you buy to eat and drink? Write a list.
EXAMPLES: *chocolate, coffee* etc.

2 Reading

Read the text below. Does it mention any of the things on your list?

Did you know...?

- It takes half an hour of swimming to burn off the calories of just one portion of chips.
- Hot dogs often have less than 25% lean meat in them.
- A can of soft drink contains about 5 teaspoonfuls of sugar.
- Some 'burger and chips' meals have over 20 teaspoonfuls of fat in them.
- In an average week British people eat a kilo of sugar in the form of sweets, soft drinks, cakes, and biscuits.
- More than six cups of coffee or tea a day could give you caffeine poisoning.

UNIT 6 Stage two

3 Discussion

'Is Fast Food Junk Food?' Find out the opinions of four other students. (Note: *junk* = rubbish, something of no value)

4 Reading

Read the leaflet advertising the benefits of eating at Kingburger restaurants.

Why, according to the leaflet, are their French fries and their milkshakes good for you?

● Understanding

Finish these sentences:

1 Kingburger restaurants base their menu on meat, bread and fish because …

2 Most of the ingredients they use in their meals come from …

3 They cook and serve their food quickly so that …

4 The only ingredient of their hamburgers is …

5 They cook their hamburgers by …

Nothing but the best

In our opinion, food should do you good as well as taste good. That's why we base our menu on nutritious foods that everyone loves: meat, bread, fish, potatoes, eggs and milk. The same kind of basics you cook with at home. As well as choosing the right ingredients, we insist on nothing but the best. Nearly all our produce comes from European Community farms. The same attention to detail applies in our kitchens too, where the food is cooked and served quickly to retain as many nutrients as possible. So whatever you choose to eat at our restaurants, you can be sure of great taste and first-class nutrition. Our hamburgers are made from prime-quality beef and nothing else. They contain no additives, fillers or extra flavourings - just 100% pure beef. And we grill our meat, so no extra fat is added in cooking. Our French fries are a valuable source of vitamin C. And one of our real dairy milkshakes will provide you with enough calcium for a whole day.

5 Vocabulary

● Food

Read the Kingburger advertisement again and make lists of words under the headings opposite:

Different foods	Things in food
meat	additives

● Cooking verbs

Use your dictionary to check the difference in meaning between these cooking verbs:

**to grill   to boil   to fry
to poach   to roast   to stew**

One word has been done for you:

to fry   *to cook in hot fat*

● Word families

Find words in the text related to these words. The first one has been done for you.

1 tasty   *taste*　　　　2 product _____

3 to add _____　4 to fill _____

5 to flavour _____　6 value _____

UNIT 6 Stage two   page 55

6 Listening

How do you think the two buildings below are connected?

Listen to the conversation to check your ideas.

7 Dictation

Listen to the conversation again and fill the gaps in these sentences.

1 Have you heard that Kingburger want to _____ the old theatre into a restaurant?
2 That _____ theatre is actually a cinema now …
3 Lots of _____ people want to turn it back into a theatre.
4 These burger companies really _____.
5 They build _____ restaurants, and …

Compare answers with a partner.

Now rewrite the five sentences without using the words in the gaps. Each new sentence should be as similar as possible in meaning to the original sentence.

8 Agreeing and disagreeing
(Language review 2, page 58)

Read the tapescript for Exercise 6 on page 148 and write a list of all the sentences in which people express opinions using the verb 'think'.

Next to each opinion write the phrases people use to agree or disagree with these opinions.

9 Discussion

Make notes expressing your opinion about these different kinds of food.

EXAMPLE: butter____good for you/natural food____

1 Diet Coke _____
2 fresh vegetables _____
3 coffee _____
4 red meat (e.g. beef) _____
5 alcohol (e.g. wine) _____
6 chocolate _____
7 fish _____
8 fried food _____

Using your notes, tell your partner what you think about these foods. Agree or disagree with each other's opinions. (Use some of the expressions in Language review 2, page 58.)

Finally, discuss which foods are the most healthy. Try to agree on the two most healthy and the two least healthy foods on the list.

Activity

Burgers or Not?

1 The situation

A well-known international company is planning to open a new burger restaurant in your town.

Why do you think some people in the town are against this plan?

2 Discussion and writing

Work in groups of four. Separate into two pairs.

Students A and B: Turn to page 142.
Students C and D: Read these instructions.

- Together with many of the residents in your town, you do not want the restaurant to open. You have different reasons for this.

  Student C
  You think burgers, chips etc. are unhealthy junk food.

  Student D
  You are against the restaurant for environmental reasons.

- Discuss your opinions with your partner. Try to agree on the arguments against the opening of this new restaurant. You want to persuade other people in the town that you are right.

- With your partner write publicity material expressing your points of view. First, decide what kind of publicity to write. Here are some ideas:

  – a leaflet to give to people in the street.
  – a poster.
  – the script for a half-minute TV video (including ideas for pictures).

3 Reporting back

Present your publicity to your small group (A, B, C and D), or to the whole class. Presentation ideas:

– Display your publicity on the classroom wall.
– Read out what you have written.
– Exchange and read the other pair's publicity.

4 Class discussion

Discuss the main arguments for and against the new restaurant plan.

UNIT 6 Activity

Language review

1 Asking for and giving opinions

These are some ways of asking people for their opinions:

What do you think about the price of food?
What's your opinion of the government?

These are some ways of expressing your opinions:

I think it's very worrying.
I believe people work too hard.
In my opinion/view they're making a lot of fuss about nothing.

These expressions stress that you are giving your personal opinion:

As far as I'm concerned,…
If you ask me,…

This is a very polite way of giving an opinion:

Don't you think smoking is bad for you?

You can also give your opinion and add a short question:

I don't think people should smoke in public, do you?
I think jogging is very bad for you. What's your opinion?/What do you think?

2 Agreeing and disagreeing

These are some ways of agreeing with someone:

Opinion	Agreement
I think it's wrong.	I (quite) agree.
I think it's a beautiful building.	So do I.
I don't think they should use it.	Neither do I./Nor do I.

These are some ways of disagreeing:

Opinion	Disagreement
I think there enough burger restaurants already.	I don't/can't agree. I don't/can't accept that. I disagree.
I think it's an ugly building.	I don't.
I don't think most people want burgers.	I do.

These two expressions are very informal and can be rude:

(That's) Rubbish!   (That's) Nonsense!

Here are two polite ways of starting an expression of disagreement:

***I'm sorry**, I disagree with you.*
***I'm afraid** I can't accept that.*

3 Pronouns: you, we and they

We often use *you*, instead of the formal *one*, to refer to people in general:

If you live or work with smokers, you can get cancer.
Where can you buy stamps in this town?

We/us often refers to people in general including the speaker:

The companies are only giving us what we want.

We often use *they/them* to refer to unknown people, especially impersonal authorities or experts:

A few years ago they had a campaign against butter.
They say if you get too much sun …

4 Compound pronouns

● **Form and meaning**

everyone/everybody	all people
everything	all things
no one/nobody	not (even) one person
nothing	not (even) one thing
someone/somebody	an unknown person
something	an unknown thing
anyone/anybody	a person, it doesn't matter who
anything	a thing, it doesn't matter what

● **Use**

All these compound pronouns are singular and take singular verbs:

Somebody is coming.
Does anyone want to watch the film on TV?

In everyday speech we often use plural pronouns and possessive adjectives with these words:

*I can hear a noise. I think someone is starting **their** car.*
*Everyone worries when **they** are learning to drive.*

In more formal speech and in writing we use singular forms:

*Somebody has left **his** keys on the table.*
*Everyone must make **his or her** own decision on this matter.*

UNIT 7
Opener

◆ With your partner, try to match these places with the names of airlines.

MEXICANA
TURKISH AIRLINES
AIR INDIA
LUFTHANSA
ICELANDAIR
BRITISH AIRWAYS
OLYMPIC AIRWAYS

◆ Which are the favourite tourist destinations in your country?
◆ Have you been abroad? Where to? Where would you like to go if you could choose? Why?

UNIT 7 Opener page 59

Stage one

Personal Experiences

1 Reading

Read the following four letters to an English family living abroad. Which one is from:

a a friend
b an ex-colleague at work
c a married couple
d members of their family

---

2 Salisbury Crescent
Bristol
6th May

Dear Chris and Barbara,
      It was so nice to get your letter; apologies for the long delay in replying.
      We're fine. Marta and I have just returned from a hectic but most enjoyable week in Canada (Ontario) where I was invited to give some lectures. We visited Toronto (from where we nipped down to see Niagara Falls), London and Kingston. Our Brazilian friend Circe moved into our house to look after the kids. She was marvellous and the kids hardly missed us at all.
      Julian popped round the other evening. He has sold his flat and car and is planning to leave the country in the near future and go to South America to work and travel.
      Hope this finds you well. Write sometime and let us know your news.
      Love to you all,
            Henry, Marta + kids

---

23 Southwood Road,
Bristol BS7 9AG
16th May

Dear Chris & Barbara,
      Sorry I haven't been in touch before. I've been really busy trying to sort out my future. I've now decided to come out to see you, possibly in August, and certainly no later than September. If you could put me up for just a few nights, I'll make sure I get something fixed up quickly. The cheapest airfare I've found so far is £310 single with Continental. Pan Am's a bit more. Does that seem reasonable?
      My brother's getting married on Saturday and I was in charge of his stag night last weekend. It was really enjoyable. As you can imagine, there was lots of rowdy singing and practical jokes! I had to help him up to bed afterwards and he's felt a bit under the weather since then.
      Take care and write soon.
            Love to you and the girls from
                  Julian

page 60   UNIT 7 Stage one

15 Fulwell Avenue
Swindon
Wilts. SN5 4RD
14th June

Hello dears,

Well, we've just got back from our trip to Scotland. We had a fortnight there and the weather was marvellous - not like last year when it poured with rain everyday! It took us eleven hours and there was traffic all the way. Dad is feeling fine now and has been out for walks and has played some golf. My blood pressure has settled down at last but I still have it checked regularly.

Before I forget, Julian phoned just before we went away. He is now definitely coming out to Mexico City in September and is really looking forward to seeing you again. He's got his visa and is going to the States first for a month's holiday and then down to visit you.

All our love and special kisses for the girls.

Mum
xxxx

7 Hobart Road,
Bristol,
18th July

Dear Chris,

Many, many thanks for your letter - at long last a chance to write back. I've been meaning to put pen to paper for ages but you know how it is!

As you've probably heard, Julian left the school at the end of last term so there have been a few changes. He seems very excited about going abroad and had a huge farewell party last weekend for about 50 people. Everyone enjoyed themselves and we're going to miss him.

Things are hectic at work but we'll soon be on holiday, thank goodness. They've been painting and decorating some of the classrooms for the last month and it should be a big improvement.

The weather has been nice for nearly two weeks now and Ruth bought some garden chairs this morning. We may even have a barbecue soon. Wish you could be there! Drop us a line if you get time. We'd love to hear from you.

Paul.

Understanding

1 In which letter

a has someone been to Scotland?
b is someone going abroad?
c has someone left a job?
d is someone planning a wedding?
e is someone feeling a bit ill?
f has someone just come back from abroad?
g is someone feeling better?
h has someone been intending to write?

2 Each letter gives some different information about Julian and his plans. Use this information to complete the table below. When you have finished, compare your notes with another student.

Julian

Last job was in a	Has got an American ....
Wants to work in	Has sold his ....
Air ticket will cost about	Leaving England in ....
Airline	Invited 50 people to ....
Spending a month in	Organised his brother's ....

UNIT 7 Stage one   page 61

2 Vocabulary

Underline the following expressions in the letters in Exercise 1 and try to guess what they mean.

Then match them with the meanings listed.

1 to nip down
2 to pop round
3 to move into
4 to be in touch with someone
5 to sort something out
6 to put someone up
7 to fix something up
8 to be in charge of something
9 to settle down
10 to look forward to something

a to make contact with
b to let someone stay
c to be responsible for something
d to arrange
e to visit someone for a short time
f to go quickly
g to enjoy the idea of something in the future
h to solve the problems of something
i to start living in
j to become calm

3 Pronunciation

It is important to get the stress right in long words in English. Listen to the following words of four or five syllables and mark the correct stress. The first one has been done for you.

1 invitation   2 impractical
3 economics   4 politician

Where do you think the stress is on the following words? Listen to the sentences on the tape to check your answers.

a enjoyable
b positively
c unbelievable
d complicated
e Argentinian
f examination
g influential
h automatic
i uncooperative
j economist

4 Past events
(Language review 2, page 68)

1 In the following sentences from the letters, the writers are referring to past events which have a connection with the present. Which words or phrases show this connection?

*Marta and I have just returned from a hectic but enjoyable week in Canada.
My blood pressure has settled down at last.*

Read the letters again and find five more sentences like these.

2 In the following sentences the writers are referring to past events which are finished. (They have no connection with the present.) Which words or phrases tell you when the events happened?

*Julian popped round the other evening.
Julian phoned just before we went away.*

Look through the letters and find five more sentences which refer to events which are finished.

5 Practice

1 Read the text of this postcard which Brendan has received from some friends. Fill the gaps with the correct form of the verb in brackets – either the Past Simple or the Present Perfect Simple.

Dear Brendan,

We _____ (be) here in New York for a week and we _____ (enjoy) every minute. Yesterday we _____ (go) to the Metropolitan Museum of Art and last Monday we _____ (see) a show on Broadway. We _____ (have) great food every day and this afternoon we _____ (buy) tickets for a baseball game. I hope I can understand it. We _____ (not visit) the Statue of Liberty yet but we're going tomorrow. I _____ (lose) my bag last night but luckily I _____ (not have) any money in it. Well, Jackie _____ (just arrive), so I'll say goodbye.

All the best,
George

2 Brendan was born in Ireland but now lives in England. Look at the prompts below and make sentences about him using either the Past Simple or the Present Perfect Simple of the verbs given. The first one has been done for you.

1 come/England – 1970
   He came to England in 1970.
2 move/Manchester – 6 years later
3 finish/school – 1982
4 go/university – 1983-1986
5 work/insurance company – 2 years
6 visit/Greece – last summer
7 have/car – 8 months
8 live/flat – 7 weeks
9 play/squash – yesterday
10 play/trumpet – a long time

6 Pairwork

Make a list of your recent experiences and arrange them in two columns: those which refer to an event which finished in the past, and those which refer to a past event which continues into or affects the present.

Now ask your partner questions about his/her recent experiences. He/she can only answer *Yes* or *No*.

EXAMPLES: *'Have you seen any films recently?'*
'No, I haven't.'

'Did you go to the party last Saturday?'
'Yes, I did.'

7 Writing

Using the information you have just written about yourself, write an informal letter to an English-speaking friend bringing him/her up to date with your news and recent experiences. Set your letter out correctly for an informal letter. Use the letters in Exercise 1 as models.

Stage two

Personal Details

1 Listening

1 Someone telephones an employment agency. Listen to the conversation and complete their details on the agency form.

Stone Employment Bureau

Name: ....
Address: ...., Lichfield............
Telephone number (Home): ....

2 You are going to hear part of the interview at the agency. Write down six words you think you might hear on the tape. Then listen and add further details to the form.

Previous full-time employment: ....
....
Previous part-time employment: ....
Education/qualifications: 3 'A' levels:
....
Language(s): ....
Hobbies/interests: ....

UNIT 7 Stage two   page 63

2 Vocabulary

1 Match the following personal details with the headings from a form.

> receptionist
> a degree in economics
> a computer course
> 7 years secondary school
> Spanish
> 3 years in a solicitor's office
> stamp collecting
> £20,000 a year

> Experience
> Education
> Languages
> Interests/hobbies
> Training
> Salary
> Qualifications
> Previous job

2 Complete the following sentences with a suitable form of the word in capitals. You have heard all the words on the tape. If you are not sure, refer to the tapescript on page 149 for Exercise 1.

EXAMPLE:
Brendan works for an ___insurance___ company in Manchester.   INSURE

1 Unfortunately there are a lot of _____ people in many countries today.   EMPLOY

2 Laura did a _____ course last year.   SECRETARY

3 I've taken the exam three times now. It's _____. I'm no good at maths.   USE

4 He was very _____ when he began his first job.   EXPERIENCE

5 Tony speaks Italian _____.   FLUENT

3 Question tags
(Language review 1, page 68)

1 Look at the examples of question tags in these sentences and try to work out how they are formed.

1 She's Italian I think, *isn't she*?
2 You've been looking for work for about six months, *haven't you*?
3 You speak French too, *don't you*?
4 He didn't take my newspaper, *did he*?
5 They shouldn't drive so fast, *should they*?
6 I can't always depend on them, *can I*?

2 Complete each of the following sentences with the correct question tag. Then practise saying them with a partner. Try to work out the most suitable intonation.

1 You couldn't give me a hand with this, _____?
2 That was a great film, _____?
3 You're not going to wear that hat, _____?
4 Ah, you took my book, _____?
5 He's bought a new car, _____?
6 I think they've gone on holiday, _____?
7 She plays the piano really well, _____?
8 We can easily finish this work today, _____?

Now listen to the tape to check your answers.

4 Present Perfect Simple and Continuous
(Language review 2-4, page 68)

● **Present Perfect Simple**

Look at these sentences and say how the first three are different from the last three.

1 Have you been to Africa?
2 She's flown all over the world.
3 I've never tried pink champagne.
4 You haven't worked for six months, have you?
5 Peter's been away from work a lot recently.
6 Have you seen my address book? I had it a moment ago.

● **How long?**

What is the difference between these three sentences? Discuss your ideas with a partner.

> *I've worked as a secretary in an engineering company.*
> *You've been looking for work for six months, haven't you?*
> *I've been staying with my parents since November.*

page 64   UNIT 7 Stage two

● **Present Perfect Continuous**

Look at these examples of this tense.

1 *It's been raining.*
2 *I've been living at home with my parents since I lost my job.*
3 *He's been smoking for ten years.*
4 *We've been waiting an hour for the bus.*

Now put a tick (√) by any of the three explanations (a, b and c) which you think are correct.

a The sentences all talk about actions which are finished. ☐

b Number 1 talks about a past action which has just finished. ☐

c Numbers 2, 3 and 4 talk about actions or situations which began in the past and are still happening. ☐

● **Present Perfect Simple and Continuous**

Look at these two sets of examples and say what the main difference is between a and b in each case.

1 a *Alex looks really dirty. He's been washing the car.*
  b *The car looks very clean. Alex has washed it.*

2 a *Claudia's been reading all morning.*
  b *Claudia's read half the book.*

5 Practice

1 Look at the pictures and make up sentences based on the information given, using *for* or *since*.

1 3.30 p.m.
2 over an hour 
3 lunchtime 
4 ages 
5 nearly 4 hours 
6 last year 

2 In pairs, talk about how long you have been doing various things in your lives. The following verbs will help you: *live, study, learn, play, work, drive, ride*, etc. Ask questions like: *How long have you been learning English?*

3 Now write six sentences about yourself talking about things you *have done* or *have been doing* this year. Compare what you have written with your partner.

6 Making questions

For each sentence make a suitable question using either *How long?* or *When?*

1 I got your letter this morning.
2 Pat has been away in Spain for two weeks.
3 I've just finished a computer course in London.
4 Colin came to stay with us last weekend.
5 John's been playing squash for years.
6 Yasmin appeared on T.V. the other night.
7 We haven't seen her for ages.
8 He's been feeling much better since he stopped smoking.

UNIT 7 Stage two

7 Practice

● **Writing about yourself**

Use the headings on the blank form to write or invent your own C.V. (curriculum vitae).

● **Interview**

Write questions to ask a partner about their C.V. Make sure you include questions on all the different sections. Compare questions with your partner. Then interview him/her and write down the answers.

● **Writing about your partner**

Using the information about your partner from the interview, write either a job reference or a profile for a school magazine.

```
First names: ..........................    Family/surname ......................

Date of birth:  Day ..................    Month ..............    Year..........

Address: ......................................................................

.................................................................................

Post code:..........................    Telephone number:....................

Education: Schools from to ....................................................

College/university from to ....................................................

Qualifications: ................................................................

Languages:.....................................................................

Experience: (Full/part-time jobs, voluntary work etc.) ......................

Interests/hobbies: ............................................................
```

Activity

A Career in Books

1 Reading

Read the text below quickly without stopping to check any words.

1 What is the purpose of the text?
2 Where do you think you might find it?

LIDDONS BOOKSHOP

Sales Manager

We have a vacancy at our new Exeter branch for a Sales Manager. The job involves coordinating all sales staff, dealing with customers and taking decisions involving stock and displays.

The successful candidate will probably have previous sales experience, some knowledge of accounting and computers, and a good appearance. Knowledge of at least one foreign language will be an advantage.

Written applications should be sent with full C.V., the names of three referees, and details of current salary to:

**Katherine Beaumont,
Head of Personnel, Liddons PLC,
176 Brantham Street,
London WC3 4SJ**

Now read the text again more carefully and find words which mean the same as the words or phrases below:

1. Someone who is applying for a job.
2. Money you earn.
3. In the past, before now.
4. A job which is available.
5. Material kept in a shop to be sold.
6. Letter applying for a job.
7. Someone who gives a reference.
8. Present.
9. Department in a company responsible for employees.
10. People who work in a company.

2 Interview

Work in groups of four.

Look at the C.V.s you wrote in Exercise 7. Choose the ones which are most suitable for the job at Liddons and interview the candidates. You should focus on the requirements specified in the advertisement. Spend some time thinking about what questions to ask and note down each candidate's answers.

EXAMPLES: *Why did you apply for this job?*
Have you had any experience with computers?
Which languages can you speak?

3 Discussion

When you have finished the interviews, discuss each candidate's performance and qualities and decide who you would choose for the job.

4 Writing

Using your notes from the interviews, write letters of acceptance or rejection to the candidates. Use the format suggested below.

LIDDONS
BOOKSHOP

Liddons PLC
176 Brantham Street, London WC3 4SJ

```
Name and address
of candidate                                Date

Dear Mr/Ms

Thank you for coming for an interview for the post
of Sales Manager at our Exeter branch. After a lot
of thought …
```

```
                   Yours sincerely,

                   Head of Personnel
```

Language review

1 Question tags

Question tags come at the end of sentences and are used to express uncertainty, surprise or emphasis.

The question they ask is negative or positive in contrast to the first part of the sentence:

You can come to lunch, (positive) *can't you?* (negative)
She isn't angry, (negative) *is she?* (positive)

Notice we use the same verb and pronoun in both parts of the sentence.

Rising intonation in the question tag indicates uncertainty, while falling intonation shows that you are sure of something.

2 The Present Perfect Simple

Form: *has/have* + past participle

We use this tense, as the name suggests, when there is a connection between the present and the past. This may be one of several kinds:

1 When an action begins in the past and continues into the present:

The weather has been nice for nearly two weeks now.
(It was nice before and is still nice now.)
My blood pressure has settled down at last.
(It's O.K. now.)
He's felt a bit under the weather since then.
(He felt ill then and he still does.)

2 To talk about past experience (in the period of someone's life up to the present):

I haven't read that book.
Have you ever been to Scotland?

(See Unit 5, Language review 2, page 49)

3 To talk about recent experience (in the period starting a short time ago and continuing up to the present):

I've been really busy. (recently)
We've just got back from our trip to Scotland. (a short time ago)

4 When we are looking back at the past from the present:

I've never tried caviar. (until now)
She's just made some tea. (It's ready now.)
I've already posted the letter. (You don't have to now.)
He hasn't phoned yet. (I expected a phone call from him before now.)

5 To talk about the present result of a past action:

The children have finished all the milk. Look!
(Their glasses are empty.)
You've bought a new jacket. (I can see it's new.)
Ouch! I've cut my finger. (It's bleeding now.)

Notice that except with *for* (+ a period of time) and *since* (+ a specific time), we don't normally use time expressions with the Present Perfect. We often understand that the speaker means recently or lately. But we can use time expressions when they refer to a period of time which continues into the present:

He's been in a really bad mood all day.
They've worked really hard this week.

3 The Present Perfect Continuous

Form: *has/have* + *been* + *doing*

EXAMPLE: *I've been trying to practise my French.*

In this unit the Present Perfect Continuous is used to refer to actions which started in the past and **are still happening** in the present:

They've been painting the classrooms for the last month.
(They're still painting them.)
Ever since then I've been staying with my parents.
(I'm still with them.)

We also use the Present Perfect Continuous to talk about actions which have recently stopped but have **a result in the present**:

You look exhausted. What have you been doing?
Something smells nice. Have you been cooking?

4 The Present Perfect Simple and Continuous

These tenses can be confusing: they both talk about periods of time from the past to the present, both talk about situations which are still true now and both can be used with *for* and *since*.

The main difference between the two tenses is that the Present Perfect Simple focuses on the **completed** activity while the Present Perfect Continuous focuses on the activity itself and its **duration**:

She's smoked a whole packet of cigarettes.
She's been smoking all afternoon. (She's still smoking.)

Sometimes there is really no difference between the two tenses:

He's felt a bit under the weather since last weekend.
He's been feeling a bit under the weather since last weekend.

page 68 UNIT 7 Language review

UNIT 8

Opener

◆ Look at these pictures of different types of transport. Which century do you think each one belongs to?

◆ In pairs discuss the advantages and disadvantages of each form of transport shown.

◆ Which form of transport do you prefer and why?

Stage one

1 Pre-listening

Look at the map and say what kind of transport is being illustrated.

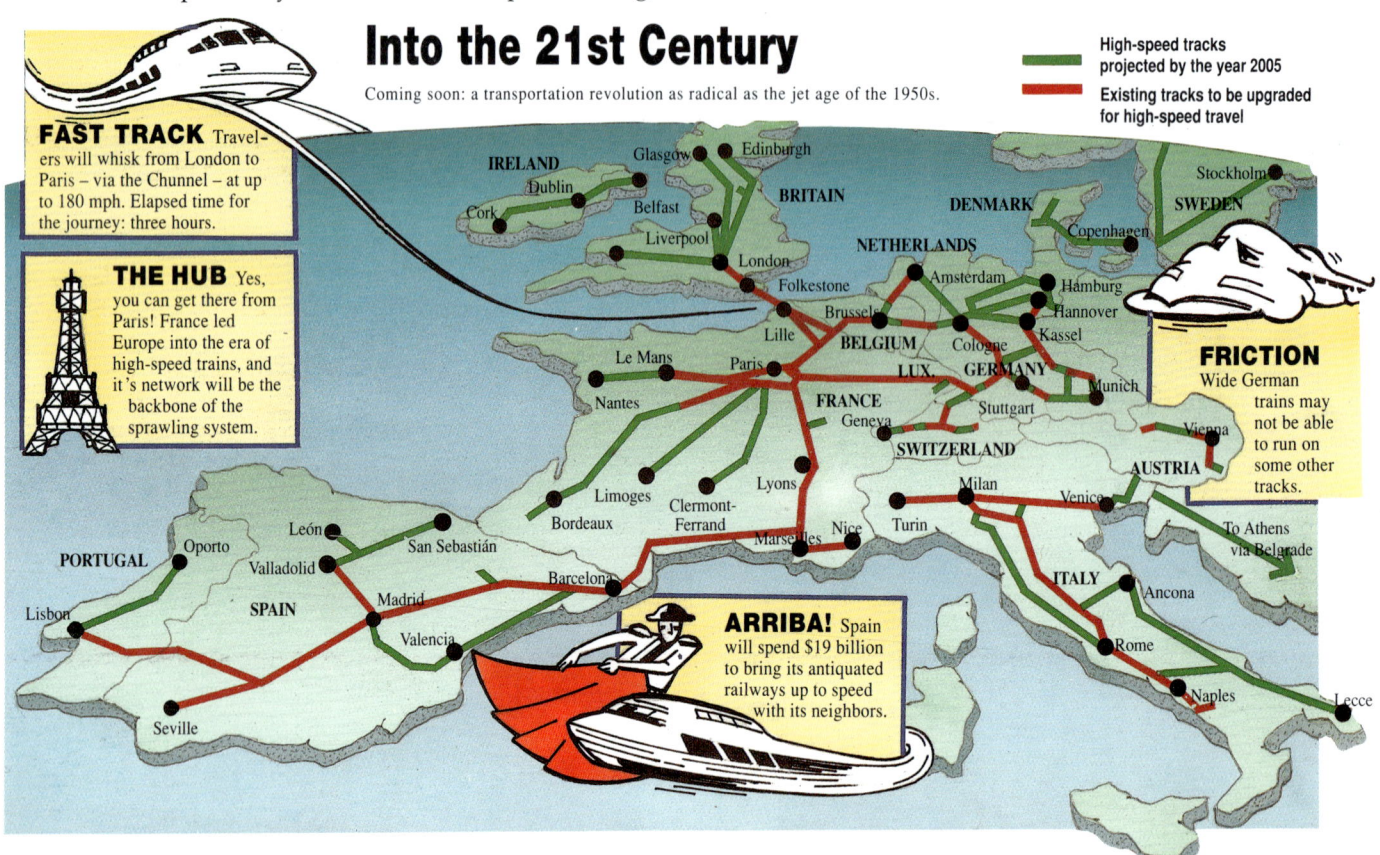

Into the 21st Century

Coming soon: a transportation revolution as radical as the jet age of the 1950s.

High-speed tracks projected by the year 2005
Existing tracks to be upgraded for high-speed travel

FAST TRACK Travelers will whisk from London to Paris – via the Chunnel – at up to 180 mph. Elapsed time for the journey: three hours.

THE HUB Yes, you can get there from Paris! France led Europe into the era of high-speed trains, and it's network will be the backbone of the sprawling system.

FRICTION Wide German trains may not be able to run on some other tracks.

ARRIBA! Spain will spend $19 billion to bring its antiquated railways up to speed with its neighbors.

In pairs, discuss the differences you think these changes will make to business, tourism and relations between countries.

What problems are suggested by the illustration?

Can you think of any similar changes being made to the transport system in your country or in another country? Describe them.

2 Listening

1 You are going to hear a telephone conversation taking place in 1999. As you listen, complete the information about Belinda's journey.

2 In pairs, work out how long each stage of the journey will take.

Then, using the distances below, calculate approximately how fast the train will be travelling for each part of the journey.

Stage 1 → 2   280 miles   _____ m.p.h.
Stage 2 → 3   240 miles   _____ m.p.h.
Stage 3 → 4   330 miles   _____ m.p.h.

1 Leave London 8:15 a.m.
2 Arrive Paris 11 a.m.
   Lunch with Jean-François.
   Leave Paris 3:10 p.m.
3 Arrive Lyons 5.15 p.m.
   Leave Lyons 5:88 p.m.
4 Arrive Barcelona around 10 p.m.
   Dinner with Carlos.

page 70   UNIT 8   Stage one

3 Vocabulary

1 Read the text and fill each space with one word from the list below.

rail   be   tunnel   apart   centre   with   major   will

Within the decade, station-to-station travel times between _____ European cities will drop dramatically. Passengers on the new high-speed trains using the new _____ under the English Channel will travel from London to Paris in just under three hours, compared _____ five today. London and Cologne will be just a bit more than four hours _____ ; Barcelona will be five hours from Paris. Scotsmen _____ be able to board a train in Edinburgh after teatime and _____ skiing in the Alps bright and early next day. European _____ traffic will quadruple between now and 2015 and airlines will almost certainly be the losers. To achieve this they will be building 4,600 miles of new track. The new rail network will put France at the _____ from which the major lines radiate.

2 Underline all the words in the text which are associated with travel.

3 Put each of the words below under one of the four headings. Some words fit more than one category.

SHIP   TRAIN   PLANE   CAR

pilot	ticket	hostess	rail
passenger	dining-car	cabin	motorway
carriage	lifeboat	driver	terminal
station	sailor	captain	port

4 The future
(Language review 1 and 2, page 77)

Look again at the text in Exercise 3. How is the future expressed? Which of these futures is being used in the text?

a Making predictions
b Deciding to do something at the moment of speaking

What do you think the difference is between these examples of the future?

1 *Passengers will travel from London to Paris in just under three hours.*
2 *They will be building 4,600 miles of new track.*
3 *He'll be starting his new job next week.*
4 *In the future many people will change careers several times in their lifetime.*

5 Practice
(Language review 1 and 2, page 77)

● **Personal predictions**

Imagine yourself in the year 2015. What will life be like? What will you be doing? Also think about what will *not* be happening, and what you will *not* be doing.

Think about all aspects of your life, and then write notes under the headings opposite:

Write sentences like this:

a *In 2015 I expect I'll be living in a small flat in Milan.*
b *I probably won't have much money.*

Now work in pairs. Compare notes with your partner. Discuss any major differences of opinion.

MY HOME
MY FAMILY
MY JOB
MY SPARE TIME

● **Offering to help**

Read the following sentences and, for each one, suggest a possible response.

1 It's dark.
2 It's a bit chilly in here.
3 This is a bit expensive, isn't it?
4 Who's that new student?
5 Someone's at the door.
6 I can't find my wallet.
7 I'm really thirsty.
8 It's too late to go to the cocktail party.

Now look at the list of responses and find the most suitable one for each statement.

a That's O.K. I'll pay.
b I'll introduce you to her, if you like.
c O.K. I'll see who it is.
d Yes it is. I'll put the light on.
e Right, I'll make some tea.
f I'll turn on the heating, shall I?
g Yes, I'll phone and tell them.
h Oh, I'll help you look for it.

Stage two

Planning Ahead

1 Reading

Look at the following pictures from two cartoon strips and put them in the right order. There are four pictures in each strip. A is the first picture of one cartoon, and B is the first picture of the other.

1 What two activities are mentioned in the cartoons?
2 What is the problem in each case?

2 Discussion

Which are your favourite cartoon characters and why?

page 72   UNIT 8   Stage two

3 Listening

It is Jenny's last day at work before a two-week holiday. She is telling her friend Diane about her plans for the fortnight.

Are the ten future events and actions mentioned by Jenny **arrangements** (planned), **intentions** (wishes) or **predictions**? Listen and decide. Write A, I or P against each item.

1 catching the ferry A
2 finding a café I
3 having breakfast I
4 the time breakfast will take P
5 meeting with Mike and Carol A
6 Dave driving A
7 Jenny driving I
8 renting a cottage A
9 cooking meals in the cottage I
10 eating in restaurants P

Compare answers with your partner. Do you agree about which events are arrangements, intentions and predictions?

Listen to the conversation again and try to agree.

4 Vocabulary

● *to catch*

To catch a bus, train, plane etc. means to be in time for and get on a vehicle to go somewhere:

Jenny and Dave are catching the early morning ferry.

When was the last time you caught a train? Where were you going?

How often have you caught a bus in the last month?

● *to go by/on*

Remember that we *go/travel* **by** *car/plane/train/bus/boat* etc., but we *go/travel* **on** *foot*.

Discuss the following questions in groups.

a How do you travel if you are going:
  to school/to work/on holiday/into your nearest town?

b What are the advantages and disadvantages of travelling by plane?

● *to drive/ride*

Notice that we **drive** *a car/a bus/a lorry* etc., but we **ride** *a bike, a horse*, etc.

5 Transport problems

Discuss these questions with your partner:

a How old do you have to be to ride a motorbike in your country? Do you have to wear a helmet?

b And a car? What kind of test do you have to take to get a driving licence in your country?

c What are the problems of riding a bike in big cities?

6 Pronunciation

In many English words we do not pronounce the letter *g* in words containing the letters *ng*.

Listen to and repeat the examples on the cassette.

Now listen to the conversation in Exercise 3 again and write down all the words which contain the /ŋ/ sound. (You may wish to look at the tapescript on page 150.)

UNIT 8 Stage two   page 73

7 Arrangements and intentions
(Language review 3, page 77)

● Arrangements
Listen again to the conversation between Jenny and Diane and look at the list you completed in Exercise 3.

Here are the first two arrangement sentences (plans that have already been made):

We're catching the early morning ferry.
We're meeting Mike and Carol just outside Paris.

Continue listening and write down the next two sentences like these.

● Intentions or plans
In her conversation with Diane Jenny says:

We're going to find a little café and have a real French breakfast.

Look at the tapescript for Exercise 3 on page 150 and find two other examples of intentions or plans.

---

8 Practice

Read Jenny's letter telling her parents about her holiday plans.

Fill each gap with a verb from the list. Think carefully about which future verb form to use – Present Continuous, *going to* or *will*.

> arrive • catch • drive
> explore • have • meet
> put up • relax • ring
> spend • start • stay • travel

Compare your answers with another student. *going to / are putting*

Home
Friday night

Dear Mum and Dad,

I thought I'd better write before we leave for France. We're really excited – it's the first holiday Dave and I have had together for nearly three years.
We **'ve spending** Monday night with some friends in Canterbury, because we **'re catching** the early morning ferry from Dover to Calais. We **'re going to** breakfast in France. I just love their coffee and croissants. I can't wait! Guy and Marie-Pierre **are putting** us **up** in Paris on Tuesday night. You remember Mike and Carol who live in Oxford? Well, we **are meeting** them near Paris on Wednesday afternoon and then we **are** all **(going to) drive/travel** on to the cottage together. Don't worry, I'**m** only **going to drive** if Dave gets tired. I've driven on the right-hand side of the road before.
Once we get there we **'re going to relax** for a couple of days and then we **'re going to explore** the area. Everyone says it's very beautiful. Altogether we **'re staying** for two weeks. We **are arriving** back on Sunday 30th and I **'m starting** my new job on the Monday morning. What an awful thought! I **'ll ring** you as soon as we get back.

Take care.

Jenny

page 74 | UNIT 8 Stage two

9 Make and do
(Language review 4, page 77)

The two couples have decided to divide up the chores while they are on holiday. Look at the two lists and choose the right verb – *make* or *do* – for each chore.

JENNY AND DAVE

_____ the hoovering
_____ the shopping
_____ the coffee
_____ the washing up
_____ the ironing

MIKE AND CAROL

_____ the beds
_____ the cooking
_____ the cleaning
_____ lunch
_____ the washing

10 Reading

Here are Jenny and Dave's plans for the fortnight of their holiday with Mike and Carol.

1 Where are they staying on their first night in France?
2 When are they arriving at the cottage?
3 What are they going to do on Friday the 21st?
4 When are they leaving the cottage?
5 When are they catching the ferry back to England?

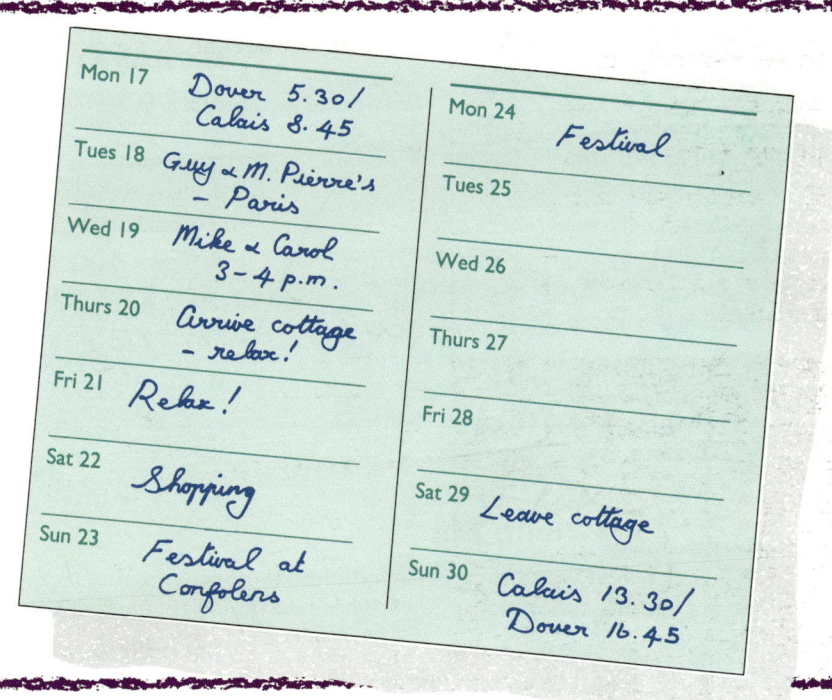

Mon 17	Dover 5.30 / Calais 8.45
Tues 18	Guy & M. Pierre's – Paris
Wed 19	Mike & Carol 3–4 p.m.
Thurs 20	Arrive cottage – relax!
Fri 21	Relax!
Sat 22	Shopping
Sun 23	Festival at Confolens
Mon 24	Festival
Tues 25	
Wed 26	
Thurs 27	
Fri 28	
Sat 29	Leave cottage
Sun 30	Calais 13.30 / Dover 16.45

11 Writing

1 Notice how the plans in Exercise 10 are written in note form.

Unimportant verbs are left out:
Guy and M. Pierre's – Paris.

Where action is important, verbs are used:
Relax!

Articles and prepositions are missed out:
Arrive cottage!

2 Now write plans for a holiday or for the next two weeks of your everyday life. Include arrangements and intentions.

3 An English-speaking friend has written saying he/she is coming to see you. Write back describing what you are doing in the next fortnight. Use the letter in Exercise 8 as a model.

Activity

Are You an Optimist or a Pessimist?

1 Reading

Do this short questionnaire to find out how optimistic or pessimistic you are.

Read each situation and choose the reaction closest to your own.

Situation 1

You see a competition in a magazine. The first prize is a new car. The three questions you have to answer to win the competition are not difficult, but you need to go to a library to find the correct answers. Do you think …?

- **A** 'I'd love to win the car. I'll go in for this competition.' ☐
- **B** 'I never win anything, so there's no point in entering.' ☑
- **C** 'If I go in for enough competitions, eventually I must win one. I think today's my lucky day.' ☐

Situation 2

You are going on a short camping holiday next week. The weather has been terrible for the last three weeks. Do you think …?

- **A** 'It's going to rain next week, there's no doubt about it. I think I'll cancel the holiday.' ☐
- **B** 'I don't really care if it rains. I'm going to enjoy the holiday anyway.' ☑
- **C** 'I'm sure the weather will be better next week.' ☐

Situation 3

You have been trying for three months to find a part-time job. You have written letters to ten possible employers, and you have had four interviews. So far you haven't got a job. Do you think …?

- **A** 'I know I'll find a job eventually.' ☐
- **B** 'It's not the end of the world if I don't get a job, but I'm going to carry on trying to find one.' ☑
- **C** 'Nobody wants me. I'm going to stop looking for a job.' ☐

Situation 4

You are taking an English exam tomorrow. You have worked very hard for the last six months and your teacher says you will pass. Do you think …?

- **A** 'I know I've worked hard, and my teacher's usually right, so I'm pretty confident about passing.' ☑
- **B** 'I hate doing exams, and I know I'm not very good at English. I'm sure I'm going to fail.' ☐
- **C** 'I hope I'll pass. I've certainly worked hard at my English.' ☐

Now check your score on page 142.

2 Listening

Look at the newspaper headlines A – D. Now listen to three radio news stories and match a newspaper headline with each of the stories.

- **A** SMOKERS AT RISK
- **B** £8 BILLION TO KEEP SEA OUT
- **C** DRUG CHIEF SENTENCED
- **D** RUSSIAN FACTORY POISONS CHILDREN

Story 1 _D_   Story 2 _B_   Story 3 _A_

3 Discussion

Work in groups of four – two optimists and two pessimists.

The radio and newspaper headlines you have just heard and read highlight some of todays most pressing problems.

How optimistic are you that we will find answers to these problems?

Invent five suitable headlines, based on your disscussions, for an English newspaper in the year 2015

UNIT 8 Activity

Language review

1 The Future with will

● Predictions

Remember that *will* + verb is used to say what we think will happen in the future, even though we are not certain:

That won't take us very long.
I expect we'll eat in restaurants three of four times

It is very common to use the following words when we make predictions:

think, expect, suppose, hope, know, to be sure, to be afraid

● Intentions

These are Jenny's last words to Julie before she leaves:

I'll send you a postcard if I remember. Bye!

She uses *will* + verb for something she has not planned or arranged, but decided to do at the moment of speaking.

We frequently use this for offers to do something. For example, Jean-François says to Belinda:

I'll give you a lift to the station.

Carlos says something similar:

I'll meet you at the station.

2 The Future Continuous

The Future Continuous – *will* + *be* + *-ing* – is used to make predictions when we are talking about continuous or repeated actions in the future:

They will be building 4,600 miles of new track.

This tense can also be used to talk about what we know we will be doing at a certain time in the future, including plans we have already made:

I'll be working all evening.
We'll be leaving around 10.30 in the morning.

3 The Future with going to and the Present Continuous

The Future with *going to* is used to talk about intentions or plans:

I'm going to drive.

The Present Continuous is used to talk about arrangements that have already been made:

We're catching the early morning ferry.
We're renting a cottage.

However it is possible in many situations to use either form. For example, there is very little difference if you say:

We're having a party next week.

or

We're going to have a party next week.

4 Make and do

These two verbs are often confused as they have very similar meanings.

Do is frequently used to talk about work:

I can't stand doing housework.
He never did any homework at school.
We'll have to do some shopping tomorrow.
There's a lot of work to do in the garden.

One meaning of *make* is to create or produce something:

Jane makes her own bread.
They used to make furniture in this factory.

Try to memorise these other common expressions with *make* and *do*:

do an exam
do someone a favour
do your best
do good
do business

make a mistake
make a mess
make a noise
make a phone call
make a suggestion
make a decision
make an excuse
make arrangements
make a plan
make the bed(s)
make money

As you can see, there are a lot more examples with *make*.

UNIT 9

Opener

◆ Look at this receipt for a family's shopping at a supermarket.

◆ Work with a partner.

1. Find four things that you cannot eat.
2. Find three kinds of food from Italy.
3. Find three non-British drinks. Where are they from?
4. How many onions did the family buy?
5. Find something that is sold in grams, not pounds.
   (Note: 1lb = 0.45 kilograms)
6. How much did this shopping cost altogether?
7. What was the most expensive item?

◆ Many items on the receipt have been abbreviated.

   EXAMPLE:

   Cauli/Broc soup = Cauliflower and Broccoli soup.

What do you think these abbreviations stand for?

- **WHT** BAGUETTE
- SWORDFISH **STKS**
- **TOM** KETCHUP
- **VEG** OIL
- **S** FLOWER **MARG**
- NATURAL **YOG**

```
J SAINSBURY PLC
    STANWAY
                              £
  JS   WHT BAGUETTE         0.74
ORANGES
       4 @ £0.20            0.80
  ONIONS
  4.09 lb @ £0.18/lb        0.74
  WHITE CABBAGE
  1.21 lb @ £0.24/lb        0.29
  JS   TAGLIATELLE          0.65
  JS   WHITE TISSUES        0.67
  BAKING POTATOES           0.72
  JS   TOOTHPASTE           0.59
  JS   MINI DONUT X6        0.49
  LEEKS
  1.09 lb @ £0.55/lb        0.60
  CAULI/BROC SOUP           0.35
  JS   EARL GREY TEA        0.64
CARROTS
       0.63 lb @ £0.29/lb   0.18
  JS   COD PORTIONS         2.59
  JS   WHOLE BEANS          0.52
  TOMATOES
  1.25 lb @ £0.64/lb        0.80
  PIZZA SLICE               0.99
  SWORDFISH STKS            3.02
  JS   BLANC LOIRE          2.55
  JS   MINERAL WATER        0.44
  TOM KETCHUP 460G          0.73
  FISCHER PILS              1.59
  JS   BLEND VEG OIL        0.54
  JS   S.FLOWER MARG        0.59
  JS   FRENCH WHITE         0.85
  JS   FRNCH RED CAN        0.85
  JS   JAFFA JUICE          0.69
  JS   PLAIN FLOUR          0.27
  VIDEO FILM                9.95
  JS   BULBS X3             0.79
  JS   NATURAL YOG          0.25
  BAKED BEANS 450G          0.26
  JS   13 AMP PLUG          0.75
  JS   LAMBRUSCO            0.95
  JS   STH/SEAS TUNA        0.56
  JS   EGGS SIZE3 X6        0.58
  MALT VINEGAR              0.38
  CREMA BEL PAESE           0.32
  JS   F/HOUSE CHEDD        1.40

  BAL DUE                  39.69

     THANK YOU FOR YOUR CUSTOM
     PLEASE KEEP YOUR RECEIPT
        IN CASE OF QUERIES
```

◆ If you were a detective or a sociologist, what would this receipt tell you about the family? Discuss your ideas with a partner.

page 78   UNIT 9 Opener

Stage one

Supermarket Shopping

1 Listening

Listen to these short, unfinished conversations overhead in a supermarket.

1 What did the people in Conversation 2 have to do yesterday?
2 Why do the people in Conversation 4 need rice?

Listen to the conversations again and fill in this chart.

Conversation	Item of Shopping	Quantity bought	Price
1	eggs	?	£1.20 a dozen
2			✗
3			✗
4		✗	✗
5		✗	
6			

2 Guess the endings

How do you think the six conversations continue? Look at the tapescript on page 150 and choose the best ending.

1 a a pound
   b an egg
   c a dozen

2 a neighbours
   b shop
   c cafe

3 a four
   b six
   c apples

4 a some rice
   b some more
   c eight more

5 a South African apples
   b apples
   c English apples

6 a the children drink
   b it costs
   c it lasts

3 Vocabulary

With a partner, think about things you can buy in containers. Look at the picture below and the receipt on page 78.

Write lists of words under these container headings:

BOTTLES   PACKETS   CARTONS   JARS   BOXES   TUBS
BAGS   CANS/TINS   TUBES

4 Some or any?
(Language review 1, page 85)

Here are some incomplete sentences from the conversations. Finish them without listening to the tape again. One of the missing words in each sentence is *some* or *any*.

1 Have _____ _____ _____ eggs? They're only £1.20 a dozen this week.

2 Yesterday, I had to _____ _____ Nescafé…

3 Shall _____ _____ _____ apples?

4 Have _____ _____ _____ English ones?

Compare your answers with a partner.

Look at the tapescript for Exercise 1 on page 150 and check your answers. Try to work out when we use *some* and when we use *any*.

UNIT 9 Stage one   page 79

5 Prices
(Language review 2, page 85)

With a partner, look back at the shopping receipt on page 78.

Ask questions like this: *How much are mushrooms?*

Give answers like this: *They're £1.32 a pound.*

6 Practice

Make a list of your favourite drinks and snacks, with the price you usually pay for each thing.

EXAMPLE:
Coke – 5 francs a can
Hamburgers – 2000 lire each
Peanuts – 100 pesetas a packet

Compare lists with your partner.
1 How many things do you both like?
2 Do you have to pay more or less than your partner?

7 Countable and uncountable nouns
(Language review 3, page 85)

Make a list of all the food nouns from the supermarket conversations. EXAMPLES: *eggs   coffee*

Write these nouns under two headings:

Things you can count   – e.g. *an egg / two eggs / a dozen eggs*
Things you can't count – e.g. *coffee*

Things you can count	Things you can't count
eggs	coffee

Add more nouns to these lists. Here are some ideas:

1 Things in your classroom   (e.g. *chair*)
2 What things are made of   (e.g. *wood*)
3 Clothes and materials   (e.g. *shirt / cotton*)
4 Liquids and gases   (e.g. *water / air*)

Compare lists with your partner.

8 How much? and How many?
(Language review 4, page 85)

You and your partner are having a party at the weekend. You have invited twenty people. Discuss what kinds of food and drink you need to buy, and then write a shopping list, like this:

Now decide how much of each type of food and drink you need to buy.
Think about quantities and containers. Make conversations like this:

A *How many bags of crisps shall we get?*
B *Let's get ten large ones.*
A *How much cheese do we need?*
B *About two kilos.*

When you have decided how much or how many you need of everything you have decided to buy, add the quantities to the list.

Compare your list and quantities with another pair of students.

9 Pronunciation

Listen to these five short conversations. The first speakers make mistakes and the second speakers correct them. Write down the words the second speakers stress.

EXAMPLE:

Tom   *I'll get some green apples, shall I?*
Ben   *No, get **red** ones.*

Now listen to these six questions. They all contain mistakes. Answer the questions and correct the mistakes. Don't forget to stress the correction.

EXAMPLE:

Question   *Pizza is from France, isn't it?*   (Italy)
You   *No, it's from **Italy**.*

10 Reading

Why did the writer of this article buy only five cigarette lighters and not ten? Read the text and find out.

Take some French Leave for Bargains
by Diane Firmin

Crossing the Channel for a day or a weekend, including a shopping expedition, is becoming more popular every year. The weeks before Christmas are especially busy as families, friends and social clubs arrange excursions to buy cheap drinks and luxury gifts such as cheeses, chocolates, paté and perfume. Other popular purchases are French saucepans and kitchenware.

A trip to Calais can be a real bargain. The price of a special day return on the hovercraft, at £10, can easily be covered by the saving on purchases.

On a recent trip, I went to the Mammouth hypermarket in Calais. I found Arabica coffee at about one third less than I would pay for good coffee in my local supermarket. Paté de Campagne was about £4 a kilo, and soft cheese with garlic and herbs was about £6 a kilo.

Sea salt was another bargain, as were my favourite Greek black olives. Olive oil was quite a bit cheaper than on this side of the Channel, and I bought several packs of four different mustards, to give as little extra presents to members of my family.

Another good buy which I discovered just as I was leaving the hypermarket was disposable cigarette lighters. The packs of ten lighters for 11 francs seemed the most popular, but, as a non-smoker, I took five, to hand round to friends.

Like the other English shoppers, I went home from my cross-Channel trip feeling well pleased with my duty-free purchases.

Read the article again and make a list of all the cheap things mentioned.

Next to each item write C if these things are countable in the text, or UC if they are uncountable. Which nouns on your list can be both countable *and* uncountable?

Understanding
1 Why do so many British people go to France before Christmas?
2 In what way could you say that the journey to France costs nothing?
3 Why do you think olive oil is much cheaper in France than in Britain?
4 Why did the writer buy more than one pack of mustards?

11 Vocabulary

1 Find words in the article which mean about the same as:

   a things you buy
   b things you use in the kitchen
   c a very big supermarket
   d something cheap

2 Find three words which mean 'a journey with a purpose'.

3 Write a list of the phrases which relate to prices and money.
   EXAMPLES: *cheap   a real bargain*

12 Talking points

Discuss these points with a partner.

What things does your country produce that foreign visitors might buy:

1 as presents to take home to their friends and family?
2 as souvenirs for themselves?
3 because they are cheaper in your country than in many other countries?

If you were going to another country to shop for bargains …

1 Which country would you visit?
2 What would you buy there?

UNIT 9 Stage one

Stage two

Valuables

1 Listening

Listen to five people giving their answers to the question:

'What's your most valuable possession?'

Which of these things are mentioned by the speakers?

- an old car ☐
- jewellery ☑
- a musical instrument ☑
- a collection ☑
- an old painting ☐
- a photograph ☑
- a piece of antique furniture ☐
- a house ☐

Listen to the cassette again and fill in the details on a chart like this:

Speaker	Possession	Value (£)
1		

2 Possessive pronouns
(Language review 5, page 86)

How could you rewrite the words in the speech bubble so that they mean the same?

What other English words are there like *mine*?

Speech bubble: "This Rolls Royce is mine"

3 Writing
(Language review 2, page 85)

Write about your most valuable possession. Here are some ideas:

1. What is your most valuable possession? (You can choose something that is worth a lot of money, or something of sentimental value.)
2. How much is it worth?
3. Describe what it looks like: How big is it? What shape is it? What is it made of? etc.
4. What can you do with it?
5. Where did you get it from?

4 Guessing game

Find out what your partner has written about. Ask questions like this:

Can you wear it? Is it made of metal? Is it small?

You can only ask ten questions. Then you must guess what the thing is. (Your partner can only answer *Yes* or *No* to your questions.)

5 Reading

Before you read the text about gold, fill in a chart like this:

GOLD: FACTS	GOLD: QUESTIONS
What I already know	What I would like to know
Gold is a soft metal.	Where does most of the world's gold come from?

Compare notes with your partner. Try to answer each other's questions.

Now read the text. Check your 'facts' and look for the answers to your questions.

Heavy Metal

1. The total amount of gold mined since the Stone Age is about 100,000 tonnes. If it was all put together, it would form a 20-metre cube, a little larger than a tennis court.
2. The world's largest collection of gold is not in Fort Knox (10,000 tonnes), but in the Federal Reserve Bank of New York, beneath the streets of Manhattan. It holds more than 40,000 tonnes.
3. Seventy-one per cent of the world's gold comes from South African mines.
4. The world's deepest gold mines are the Western Deep Levels in Carleton, South Africa, at 12,390 feet.
5. Gold is so soft that a 24 carat piece as big as a matchbox could make enough gold leaf to cover a tennis court. It would be less than 1/10,000th of a millimetre thick.
6. The most valuable religious object in the world is a fifteenth-century gold Buddha at the Wat Trimitr Temple Bangkok. It weighs five-and-a-half tons and is ten feet tall. It is worth $28,500,000.
7. The largest gold nugget ever found was the Holtermann nugget from the Star of Hope mine in Australia. It contained 220 lb of gold.
8. The biggest theft of gold bullion was the Brinks Mat robbery at Heathrow Airport on November 26th 1983. Six masked men removed 6,000 bars of gold worth a total of £26,369,778.

● **Reading for detail**

Fill the gaps in these sentences with information from the text.

1. 40% of the gold in the world is in _____.
2. There was 220lb of gold in _____.
3. The Western Deep Levels are the _____ in the world.
4. The value of the gold stolen from Heathrow Airport in 1983 was _____.
5. There are 10,000 tonnes of gold in _____.

6 Pronouns
(Language review 6, page 86)

Read these two sentences from the Exercise 1 recording:

My saxophone cost me £600 two years ago.
My Rolls Royce. I bought it in 1959.

Make a list of other pronouns like *me* and *it* that often follow verbs.

Now read this sentence:

That's my mother's gold ring. My father gave it to her for Christmas.

With a partner think of some more sentences like this.

7 Vocabulary

● **Measurements**
(Language review 7, page 86)

Look through the text and find:

a. three phrases which say how heavy something is.
b. a phrase which says how deep something is.
c. a phrase which says how thick something is.

● **Nouns and adjectives**

Which adjectives are related to these nouns? (Some of the adjectives are in the text.)

a depth _____   d softness _____

b thickness _____ e length _____

c width _____   f weight _____

UNIT 9 Stage two

Activity

Amusements?

1 Discussion
Work in pairs.

Look at the picture and then discuss these questions.

1 What are these young people doing?
2 Do you ever do this?
3 What other kinds of gambling are there?

2 Reading

Read this short text about Jason. Why is he now in prison?

> Seven years ago, when Jason was eleven, he put five 10p pieces into a fruit machine in a café. He won £10. He never won another jackpot, but he was hooked. He is now in prison.
> His addiction made him stay away from school and steal from his parents. Worse than than, he attacked an old lady and stole the £2.35 she had in her purse.
> Jason is now serving a prison sentence for robbing the old lady.

Use a dictionary to check the meanings of these words from the text.

a fruit machine   b jackpot   c hooked   d addiction   e sentence

3 Discussion
Work in groups.

- What is Jason's problem?
- Is prison the best place for people like Jason?

4 Listening

Listen to this extract from a radio phone-in programme. Where does Charlie get his money from? If you were the Presenter of this phone-in programme, what advice would you give to Charlie? Your advice can be in speech or in the form of a personal letter.

5 Poster

Design a poster to warn young people of the dangers of spending money on fruit machines.

Language review

1 Some and any

● Some

We use *some* to refer to quantities when the exact amount or number is not important:

*I had to borrow some coffee from the neighbours yesterday.
Shall we get some apples?*

We also use *some* to mean 'not all':

*We used some of the eggs to make an omelette.
Some sports are dangerous, but most are quite safe.*

● Any

Use *any* in negative sentences to mean 'no':

*We haven't got any eggs. (= We have no eggs)
I haven't got any money. (= I have no money)*

Use *any* in questions when you are not sure whether the things you are talking about exist or not:

*Did you buy any souvenirs when you were in America?
Have we got any bread?*

Use *any* in positive sentences to mean 'all' or 'it doesn't matter which one or what type':

Pepsi and Coke taste the same to me. In fact I like any cola drink. (= all cola drinks)

● *Some* and *any* as pronouns

We can use *some* or *any* without nouns:

*'Can you lend me some coffee?' 'I'm sorry we haven't got **any** ourselves.'
'Do we need any rice?' 'No, we've still got **some** at home.'*

2 Prices, quantities and values

These are all ways of talking about prices and quantities:

*How much are onions?   They're 18p a pound / 40p a kilo.
How much is mineral water?   It's (only) 62p a bottle.
What does a can of Coke cost?   About 20p. / 80p for a pack of six.
Are the grapefruit expensive?   Yes, they're 30p each.*

Use the word *worth* to talk about value:

How much is the Mona Lisa worth?   It's worth at least £50 million.

3 Countable and uncountable nouns

Countable nouns are nouns that have singular and plural forms:

a person a house a town a country

You can count these nouns:

two people three houses ten towns 12 countries

Uncountable nouns (mass or 'stuff' nouns) have no plural form:

bread air water money music love

You cannot count these. (You **cannot** say: *two breads* or *ten waters*.)

Talk about quantities of uncountable nouns like this:

two pieces of bread ten glasses / litres of water

Some nouns are countable and uncountable, but with different meanings:

a chocolate	*I bought my mother a box of chocolates for her birthday.*
chocolate	*Chocolate makes you fat.*
a coffee	*Can I have two coffees, please. (= 2 cups of coffee)*
coffee	*If I drink coffee at night, I can't sleep.*
cheese	*I really love cheese.*
cheeses	*We bought five different cheeses in France. (= varities of cheese)*

4 Many, much, a lot of

Many and *much* are used mainly in negative sentences and questions:

*There aren't many eggs left.
Is there much tea left?*

Many is used with plural countable nouns:

*There aren't many cars on the road tonight.
How many guests have you invited to your party?*

Much is used with uncountable nouns:

*There isn't much traffic on the road tonight.
How much food have you bought for the party?*

A lot of ... is used (in positive statements) with countable and uncountable nouns:

*A lot of cars use unleaded petrol these days.
You've bought a lot of bread for the party, haven't you?*

UNIT 9 Language review

5 Possessive adjectives and pronouns

These words are possessive adjectives:

my your his her our their

They are always used with a noun:

Have you met my mother?
He can't find his car keys.

These words are possessive pronouns:

mine yours his hers ours theirs

They are used instead of nouns:

That isn't John's car. It's mine.
Mike's house is too big. I prefer ours.

6 Object pronouns

An object pronoun is a pronoun used as the object of a verb:

me you him her it us them

There are two kinds of object pronouns:

Direct object pronouns:

There's my brother. Have you met him before?
I've lost my keys. Have you seen them?

Indirect object pronouns:

Julia has written this letter to me.
Have you seen Bob? I lent him a record.

Sentences can have a direct and an indirect object pronoun:

He sent it to me. (He sent me it.)
He bought them for her. (He bought her them.)

Notes:

1 The indirect object with *to* or *for* comes after the direct object.
2 The indirect object without *to* or *for* comes before the direct object.
3 We use *to* + the indirect object pronoun with some verbs:

   give, lend, offer, pay, sell, show, take, teach, write

4 We use *for* + the indirect object pronoun with other verbs:

   buy, fetch, get, make, order

7 Measurements

Notice these ways of talking about dimensions and weight:

Depth   *How deep are the mines in Carleton? They're 12,390 feet deep.*
Weight   *How heavy was the Holtermann nugget? It was 220lb. How much did the Holtermann nugget weigh? It weighed 220lb.*
Size   *How tall is your brother? He's nearly 2 metres tall. How long is the River Nile? It's 4,145 miles long.*
Width   *How wide is the Nile Delta? It's 190 km wide.*
Height   *How high is Mount Everest? It's 8,800 metres high.*

Talking about percentages:

71 per cent (%) of the world's gold comes from South Africa.
Women make up 52% (per cent) of the population.

page 86   UNIT 9 Language review

UNIT 10 Opener

◆ Look at the photographs with your partner. What special skills or abilities do these animals have?

EXAMPLE: *Spiders make webs.*

◆ What other animals do you know with special skills?

◆ What abilities and skills do human beings have that animals do not?

UNIT 10 Opener

Stage one

Survival

1 Reading

Read this introduction to the Baka people.

What kind of people are the Baka?

Cameroon is one of the most varied countries in Africa. In a population of eight million, there are more than 200 races, most with their own language and culture. In the north the climate is hot and dry, but the south-eastern corner is covered in thick tropical rainforest. This is the home of the Baka Pygmies. The Baka depend on the forest for their survival; it provides them with building materials, medicines and all their food. The Baka know how to make the best use of everything they find. In the wet season they have to leave their villages and go into the forest to find food.

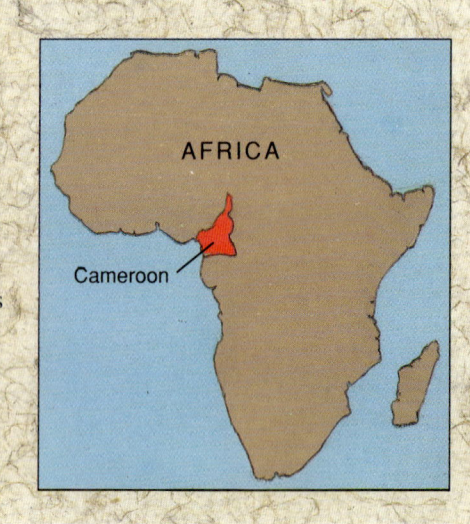

Now match these photographs (A-D) with the paragraphs of text.
One paragraph is not illustrated

1. The Baka perform the Fire Dance, to cure illnesses. The dancer or 'doctor' warms his hands in the fire and then puts them on the part of the body that is ill.

2. Honey from the African Honeybee is the food the Baka value above all. Usually the bees' nests are high above the ground, so collectors have to climb the giant trees to collect the honey.

3. In Baka society, the women are responsible for building huts from young trees and leaves. It is also their job to gather vegetables, collect water and do the cooking. The men have to provide meat and collect honey. Men and women share the job of bringing up the children.

4. At the beginning of the dry season, the level of water in the streams falls. This is the best time for dam fishing. Groups of women dam the streams at the narrowest point so that below the dam the water becomes very shallow. Then they can easily catch small fish, crabs and shrimps.

5. The Baka's most remarkable skill is their ability to understand the chemistry of the forest. They can detoxify plants which are naturally inedible by cooking and other processes. They also know how to use chemicals for hunting. For example, they use plant poison on arrows which they shoot from crossbows to kill monkeys.

page 88 UNIT 10 Stage one

2 Reasons

With a partner, discuss possible answers to these questions. (The answers are *not* given in the texts.)

1 Why is the wet season the best time for the Baka people to find food?
2 Why do they leave their villages to look for food?
3 Why is honey so important to the Baka?
4 Why are the bees' nests so high in the trees?
5 Why do the women catch fish and gather vegetables, while the men hunt and collect honey?

3 Vocabulary

● **Matching**

Match each of these verbs from the texts with an appropriate noun. Then make a sentence using both words. Follow the example.

● **Opposites**

Find the opposites of these adjectives in the texts.

1 healthy 2 old 3 wet 4 worst
5 widest 6 deep 7 edible

Verb	Noun	Sentences
EXAMPLE: to cure	huts	Doctors cure illnesses.
1 to climb	fish	
2 to catch	vegetables	
3 to dam	dances	
4 to gather	illnesses	
5 to perform	trees	
6 to build	streams	

4 Abilities

(Language review 1, page 94)

Read texts 1-5 again. As you read, make a list of things that the Baka people can do.

Scan the texts again for expressions which tell you about the Baka people's abilities.

Can, know how to, have the ability to are three ways of talking about abilities or skills. Here are some more examples:

1 *I can drive a car, but I can't ride a bicycle.*
2 *My brother knows how to programme a computer.*
3 *She has an amazing ability to see in the dark.*

What is the difference between the form of the infinitives in Sentence 1 and Sentences 2 and 3? Compare your answer with a partner.

5 Listening

You are going to hear someone talking about child development between the years of five and eleven. Before you listen, look at this list of abilities and, next to each, write the age at which you think most children can do these things.

Abilities	Age	
	Your guess	Actual
Catch a ball		6
Climb		5
Do gymnastics		7
Hit a ball		6
Juggle		8-10
Jump		5
Ride a bicycle		7
Ride a tricycle		5
Run		5
Skip		6
Swim		8-10
Swing by the arms		6
Throw a ball		5
Do trampolining		7

Now listen to the recording and make a note of the actual ages.

UNIT 10 Stage one   page 89

6 Vocabulary

What are the differences in meaning between these pairs of verbs?

1 run / skip
2 climb / jump
3 throw (a ball) / hit (a ball)
4 balance / juggle

7 Can
(Language review 2, page 94)

What is the difference in the use of *can* in these two sentences from the recording?

There can be a great variation in children's height and weight.
At around five years, most children can run, climb, jump, ride …

Compare ideas with a partner.

8 Personalised practice

Write a list of your skills and abilities. Which five are you most proud of?

Next to each ability write the age at which you could first do these things.

Now work in pairs. Ask your partner whether he/she can do the same things.

EXAMPLES:

Can you speak French?
Do you know how to use a typewriter?
When did you learn to skateboard?

Write the answers on a chart like this:

Abilities	Your age	Your partner	
1 Speak French	14	√	12
2 Use a typewriter	12	X	--
3 Skateboard	9	√	9
4			

Compare charts with your partner. Talk about some of the things you can both do.

9 Necessity
(Language review 3, page 94)

Answer these questions about the Baka people. Try to remember the answers without looking back at the texts.

1 What do the Baka people do in the wet season?
2 How do the Baka men collect honey?
3 The Baka women gather vegetables, collect water and do the cooking. What do the men do?

Now look back at the texts. Which verb shows that the above actions are necessary?

Now answer these questions about the Baka people.

4 Who has to build huts?
5 Who has to bring up the children?
6 Why do they have to detoxify plants?

10 Had to
(Language review 3, page 94) ← not yet

Compare the everyday lives of ordinary people in your country 200 years ago with the lives of people today.

EXAMPLES:

Two hundred years ago, everyone had to wash their clothes by hand.
Two hundred years ago, children didn't have to go to school.

Compare ideas with a partner.

11 Writing

Write a letter to some British friends who are planning to visit you in your country. Tell them some of the things they will have to do or won't have to do.

EXAMPLES:

Don't forget you will have to drive on the right-hand side of the road.

You won't have to bring an umbrella because it hardly ever rains.

page 90 UNIT 10 Stage one

Stage two

Life is Hard

1 Listening

Listen to four short conversations. Match each one with a situation from this list by putting the number in the correct box.

Talking about a visit ☐
Redecorating a kitchen ☐
Buying a coat ☐
Buying new shoes ☑ 2
Looking for a flat to rent ☐ 4
Talking about a car accident ☐ 1 *must*
Talking about a phone conversation ☐ 3 *must*
Talking about a broken garage light ☐

Compare answers with a partner. Give reasons for your choices.

2 Listening and guessing

Listen to the four conversations again and guess or work out the answers to these questions.

Conversation 1
a Who is *he*?
 (*He'll see the damage ...*)
b What is *it*?
 (*... gets it out of the garage*)
c What is *the damage*?

Conversation 2
d Why do you think the customer asks the assistant not to wrap up what she has bought?

Conversation 3
e What is the relationship between the two speakers?
f Who do you think *he* is?
 (*I'll get him to ring me ...*)

Conversation 4
g What does the speaker mean by *the rest of it*?
h What is the relationship between the two speakers?

3 Phrasal verbs: get

In Conversation 2 the shop assistant says:

 '*How are you getting on?*'

This means: '*Are you all right?*' or '*Do you need any help?*'

Rewrite sentences 1-6, keeping the meaning as similar as possible but replacing the phrasal verb.

EXAMPLE: I wrote to him three weeks ago but he hasn't got round to answering.

 I wrote to him three weeks ago, but he hasn't found time/taken the trouble/bothered to answer.

1 My exam is next Wednesday, so I'm working very hard. It's really getting me down.
2 I've known Mike since I was five years old, and we still get on very well.
3 I'm so busy. I'd like to get out of my meeting tomorrow.
4 It often takes a long time to get over a heart attack.
5 I've been shopping all day. I've got through at least £100.
6 Why don't you get rid of that old jacket? It looks terrible.

4 What is wrong?

Rearrange these words to make captions for the two cartoons.

shoes me are these too for small

isn't big people kitchen for this enough two

Now look around the room you are in now. What is wrong with it? Make a list of comments like these:

 The lights are too bright.
 The room isn't big enough for twenty students.

UNIT 10 Stage two   page **91**

5 Pronunciation

The mixture of stressed and unstressed words or syllables (parts of words) gives English its rhythm.

Listen to and repeat two short extracts from the conversations.

Listen again and write the two sentences.

Now listen and mark the stresses like this:

■ ■
We're going up to London on Friday.

Listen to five more sentences with the same rhythm. Write them down and then mark the stresses.

Discuss these questions with a partner.

1 What kinds of words have stresses?
2 What kinds of words do not have stresses?
3 When people speak, what happens to these unstressed words?

6 Must or have to?
(Language review 4, page 94)

Look at these two sentences from the conversations:

You must offer to pay for a new one.
I have to pay the bills; you don't.

Which of the sentences expresses the speaker's opinion, and which expresses a fact?

Write five more sentences with *must*.

EXAMPLE:
I must phone my brother this evening.

Write five sentences with *have to*.

EXAMPLE:
I have to pay the rent on my flat tomorrow.

7 Mustn't or needn't
(Language review 5, page 94)

Read these two short dialogues:

1 'I must phone my parents to say I'm going to be late home.'
 'You mustn't phone them now. You'll wake them up.'

2 'I must phone my parents to say I'm going to be late home.'
 'You needn't phone them. I've already told them.'

What is the difference in meaning between *You mustn't phone them* and *You needn't phone them?*

Compare ideas with a partner.

8 Practice
Work in pairs.

Write a list of five things you must do in the next few days, and decide when you must do them.

EXAMPLE:

!!! DON'T FORGET !!!

Birthday present for John Friday
Book tennis court Monday

Now tell your partner the things you must do and when you must do them.

EXAMPLE: *I must buy John's birthday present on Friday.*

When your partner tells you what he/she has to do in the next few days, think of reasons why he/she needn't do these things until later, or why he/she must do them earlier.

Make conversations like this:

A *I must buy John's birthday present on Friday.*

B *You needn't buy the present on Friday. It isn't John's birthday until next month.*

or

B *You must buy it today. His birthday's tomorrow.*

page 92   UNIT 10 Stage two

Activity

School Rules

1 Reading

Which of these English secondary school rules do you think are normal and which do you find surprising?

```
                    To All Pupils

1   You must wear school uniform at all times. You must not wear
    jeans or trainers, large earrings or make-up.

2   Don't bring any of these things to school: knives, chewing-gum,
    cigarettes, matches, radios, personal stereos, or anything
    dangerous.

3   These rooms are out-of-bounds when there is no teacher present:
    laboratories, workshops, typing rooms, Home Economics rooms.

4   Pupils must bring their own equipment to every lesson.

5   You must stay at school at lunchtime unless you go home for
    lunch.

6   When you are moving between rooms or buildings, you must walk,
    not run. Remember to keep to the left.

7   Late arrivals must report to the school office.

8   Keep the school tidy at all times.

9   Don't leave money, watches or other valuables in the classroom.
    Give them to a teacher or don't bring them to school.

10  If you want to bring a bicycle to school, you must have a
    permit.
```

2 Role play

You are on a committee to make the rules for a new school or college in your town. The committee includes representatives of students, teachers and parents. Here is the agenda:

```
School Rules Committee
       Agenda

1 Clothing

2 Banned objects

3 Behaviour in school
  buildings
```

- Decide which of these groups you want to represent:

    A – Students at the school   B – Teachers   C – Parents

    Get together with other representatives of your group and try to agree on five acceptable rules and write them down.

- Now form groups of three – a Student, a Teacher and a Parent.

    You should each read out the five rules agreed by your interest group. Try to agree on five rules for the new school/college.

- Write these five rules in language which the students at the school or college will find clear and simple to understand.

UNIT 10 Activity   page 93

Language review

1 Ability

● Can

We use *can* to talk about people's abilities.

Can has only two forms:

Present Simple: *can* (all persons):
I can play the piano, but I can't play the guitar.

Past Simple: *could* (all persons):
He couldn't start his car, so he came by bus.

● To be able to

This means the same as *can*, but has all forms, including:

Future: *will be able to*:
I'm learning French, so that when I go to France I'll be able to understand what people are saying.

Present Perfect: *have been able to*:
He hasn't been able to walk since the accident.

Infinitive: *to be able to*:
You'd like to be able to swim, wouldn't you?

In the Present and Past Simple tenses, *to be able to* is a more formal alternative to *can* or *could*.

● Know how to / have the ability to

Here are some more ways of talking about abilities:

More and people these days know how to use a word processor.
Many politicians have the ability to work for twenty hours a day.

2 Can: summary of meanings

● Ability
I can speak Russian.

● Possibility
There can be a great variation in children's height and weight. (This is quite possible.)

● Permission
Can I borrow your bike?
I can't come out this evening. My father won't let me.

3 Necessity

● Have to

We use *have to* talk about something that is necessary.

Present Simple:
Baka men have to climb high trees to collect honey.

Past Simple:
It was foggy, so we had to drive very slowly.

Present Perfect:
She has had to wait all morning to see the doctor.

Future:
Will you have to work late this evening?

● Have got to

We can use *have got to* instead of *have to*:
I've got to go to the dentist tomorrow.

It suggests that the necessity is very strong.

● Must

Must is another verb used to talk about necessity.

It has only one form. We use this to talk about present and future necessities.

Present:
You must leave now. It's very late.

Future:
I must go to the bank tomorrow. I haven't got any money left.

We often use *must* in rules or laws:
You must wear school uniform at all times.

4 Must or have to?

Often it does not matter whether we use *must* or *have to*. But sometimes there is a difference.

We use *must* to refer to the opinions or feelings of the speaker:
You must offer to pay for a new one.
(The speaker thinks this is the right thing to do.)

We use *have to* refer to facts rather than matters of opinion:
In the wet season the Baka have to leave their villages.

5 Mustn't, needn't and don't have to

Mustn't and *needn't* are both opposite in meaning to *must*.

Mustn't means it is necessary *not* to do something. (You have no choice):
You mustn't drink and drive. It's against the law.

Needn't means it is *not* necessary to do something. (You have a choice):
You needn't drive home tonight. You can stay here if you like.

Don't have to is similar in meaning to *needn't*:
It's Saturday tomorrow, so we don't have to get up early.

UNIT 11

Opener

◆ Look at the comic strip and the sentences describing the story. Match each sentence with the correct frame (A-K) of the comic strip.

1 Frank told Joe he needed his help. D
2 Lacey said he had some information. A
3 Danny told Lola to shut up. F
4 Joe agreed to help Frank. D
5 Frank told Danny he wanted the diamond. H
6 Lola said she was bored. E
7 Frank said they would look after the diamond for them. K

◆ What famous fictional detectives or crime-busters do you know? Which one is your favourite?

Stage one

News Reports

1 Reading

Look at the title of the newspaper article and the photo. Which of the following words you would expect to find in the article?

guilty	luxury	traffic
restaurant	media	prison
slap	defendant	sentence
police	assault	staff
news	officer	jury
verdict	licence	sexy
court	outrageous	arrest
accused	jail	trial

Now read the article quickly for a general idea of the story. Tick (√) all the words in the list which appear in the article.

Gabor plans a gourmet life in jail

In the end, it was the jury who had the last word in the trial of Zsa Zsa Gabor. She was found guilty of committing an assault on a police officer.

Gabor – 72, 68, or perhaps 59 years old – faces a possible 18-month sentence for slapping a large traffic policeman who had stopped her car near her Bel Air home last June. She was also found guilty of driving without a valid licence and of having an open bottle of bourbon in her glove compartment.

She said, after the verdict, that she was going to write a book in prison and have three meals a day sent in from a fashionable Beverly Hills restaurant if she was sent down.

'I'm very disappointed,' she said. 'I can't believe in a country as great as ours that a 6 feet 4 inch policeman can beat up a lady of 5 feet 4 inches and use dirty language like you were a streetwalker.'

Jury foreman, John Burke, 35, told reporters 'I feel good about our decision. I'm glad it's all over.' Other members of the jury said they had tried to ignore the outrageous remarks with which Gabor had peppered her trial and the hundreds of news people who had accompanied her. They said they had also disregarded much of her testimony as inconsistent.

Gabor will be back to hear her sentence in two weeks' time. She also faces a hearing on possible contempt of court for violating an order by the judge banning her from talking about the trial while it was in progress. Staff at the Beverly Hills municipal courthouse said the past two weeks had been the strangest they had known.

In court Gabor alleged that Officer Paul Kramer had dragged her across the boot of her Rolls-Royce after arresting her. She later said she thought he was 'gorgeous and sexy'.

After the verdict, a police spokesman read a statement to the cameras on the courthouse steps, saying that officers would remain dedicated to the principle that no-one was above the law.

(Miss Gabor was sentenced to three days' imprisonment.)

● **Reading for detail**

1 Now read the article again and complete this record form.

Name of defendant:	Age of defendant: ....
Defendant lives in:	Height of defendant: ....
Defendant accused of:	Verdict of jury: ....
Arresting officer:	Possible sentence: ....

UNIT 11 Stage one

2 Are the following statements true or false? Circle the letter T or F.

1 No-one is quite sure how old Zsa Zsa Gabor is. T/F
2 She hit a traffic policeman with her car. T/F
3 She may go to prison for 18 months. T/F
4 She's planning to go to a restaurant after the trial. T/F
5 The jury said her evidence was precise and accurate. T/F
6 The judge told her not to speak to the press during the trial. T/F
7 Zsa Zsa accused Officer Kramer of assaulting her. T/F
8 She thought the Officer was very handsome. T/F

2 Vocabulary   *Homework*

1 Find words or phrases in the text which mean the same as the ones given below.

Paragraphs 1 to 3
   a twelve citizens who decide a court case
   b a physical attack   c a jury decision
   d a place for criminals

Paragraphs 4 to 6
   e amazing/shocking   f legal process   g evidence
   h punishment   i employees

Paragraphs 6-8
Try to work out what these words mean from the context.
   j violating   k banning   l alleged   m gorgeous
   n spokesman

2 Complete the sentences with one of these 'legal' words from the article. If the word is a verb, put it into the correct tense.

   arrest innocent verdict judge prison violate
   commit guilty jury police trial sentence

a Ms Gabor was on trial for _____ an assault and a traffic violation.
b She was found _____ of all the charges.
c The _____ decided on the verdict.
d She could go to _____ for 18 months.
e She has to go back to court for the _____.
f Officer Paul Kramer was the one who _____ her.
g She _____ a court order not to talk to the media during the _____.

3 Match these verbs with the appropriate nouns. Then write down the name of the person who commits these crimes. Note that some verbs can be used with more than one noun.

	Verbs	Nouns	Person
EXAMPLE:	to forge	cheques, documents	forger
1	to pick	a plane, train	
2	to steal	a bank, shop	
3	to kidnap	someone's pocket	
4	to rob	jewelry, money	
5	to hijack	a person	

3 Direct speech
(Language review 1, page 103)

Look at these examples of direct speech in pairs or groups.

> 'I'm very disappointed,' she said.
>
> Jury foreman, John Burke, 35, told reporters *'I feel good about our decision. I'm glad it's all over.'*
>
> 'I've never done anything dishonest in my life,' he shouted.
>
> When asked about the missing millions, Lady Walton said *'I know nothing about this matter.'*

1 What do these sentences have in common?
2 How do we know that we are reading exactly what someone said?
3 Where do you think you might find this kind of language?

4 Reported speech
(Language review 2, page 103)

Now compare the same examples in reported speech.

> She said she was very disappointed.
>
> Jury foreman, John Burke, 35, told reporters he felt good about their decision and he was glad it was all over.
>
> He shouted that he had never done anything dishonest in his life.
>
> When asked about the missing millions, Lady Walton said she knew nothing about that matter.

What do you think are the main differences between direct and reported speech? Think about the tenses, word order, pronouns and punctuation.

5 Practice

1 Read the article on page 96 again and underline three examples of reported speech. In pairs, try to work out what was actually said by the person.

To help you, look at this extract from paragraph 5:

> Other members of the jury said they had tried to ignore the outrageous remarks with which Gabor had peppered her trial and the hundreds of news people who had accompanied her.

> Other members of the jury said *'We tried to ignore the outrageous remarks with which Gabor peppered her trial and the hundreds of news people who accompanied her.'*

2 Look at the pictures below and match each picture with one of the reported sentences. Compare your answers with a partner. Then write in the bubbles the words the people actually said.

1 He said he'd had a very busy day at the office.
2 She said the bus was a bit late.
3 They told him they'd lost their ball.
4 She told him the soup was cold.
5 They said they thought the baby was asleep.

6 Pronunciation

Listen to the six words on the tape and repeat them.

Now listen to these six sentences and repeat them.

1 Oh, what a beautiful vase!
2 I don't like a big breakfast.
3 They've never been to Venice.
4 Ben's visiting his brother.
5 That was a marvellous barbecue.
6 Oh dear. I've broken the hoover.

7 Listening

Listen to extracts A-F and match them with these newspaper reports.

F 1 The Health Minister, Mrs Margaret Curtis, told a press conference she had no plans to resign.
A 2 When asked if he had broken into the jeweller's, Gibbons admitted that he had.
B 3 After several hours, the police told the demonstrators to disperse.
C 4 Matt Brown, United's manager, told reporters he had nothing to say about the absence of Gary Potter from the team to play Liverpool on Saturday.
D 5 There were long queues on the M25 yesterday, and motoring organisations advised motorists to use alternative routes.
E 6 Sonny 'Dynamite' Leonard said he was ready to fight world heavyweight champion Mike Clayson whenever the champion was ready.

page 98 UNIT 11 Stage one

8 Interview

Use a table like this one to note down the details of an incident when you had a problem with authority: a teacher, boss, parent etc.

Now work in pairs and try to find out as much as possible about your partner's incident. Ask questions like these:

- When did the incident happen?
- What were you doing?
- Did you feel guilty/nervous?
- What did you say to your teacher/boss?

Note down your partner's answers on the same table and compare them with your own.

	You	Your Partner
When incident took place:		
What you were doing:		
Who you had trouble with and why:		
How you felt:		
What happened:		

9 Writing

Write an account of one of the incidents you talked about in Exercise 8. Choose either yours or your partner's. Try to write what was said in the incident, using the same kind of language (direct speech and reported speech) which you practised from the newspaper article.

Stage two

Messages and Excuses

1 Listening

Listen to each of the messages left on an answerphone and match them with the headings in the list.

- a Refusing to do something
- b Apologising/making an excuse
- c Giving advice
- d Making a suggestion
- e Reminding someone about something
- f Giving someone a warning

How many of the messages are not from friends? How do you know?

● Understanding

Listen to the telephone messages again and say if these statements are true or false. Circle the letter T or F.

1. Jim Tate is going to give Paul a lift. T/F
2. Paul has a dental appointment this week. T/F
3. Mr Davies wants a new contract. T/F
4. Paul lives at number 17. T/F
5. Mr Haynes is upset about Paul's dogs. T/F
6. Phil can play squash on Saturday. T/F
7. Sarah can't come to lunch at Paul's because she's going to her mother's. T/F
8. She wants Paul to phone her. T/F

2 Vocabulary

● Out of action

Rewrite the sentences without using the phrases in italics. Is there any difference in meaning between these phrases?

EXAMPLE: Jim Tate's car is *out of action*.
Something is wrong with Jim's car.

1. My car *broke down* on the way home yesterday.
2. Oh no. The lift is *out of order* again.
3. This phone *doesn't work*.
4. One of the engines was seriously *defective*.
5. The main problem with the computer was a *faulty* transformer.

UNIT 11 Stage two   page 99

● **Expressions with** *keep*

Paul's neighbour asks him to *keep* his dog *under control*.

Complete these sentences with the correct preposition from the list:
to, up, away, out, in, on, down.

Check your answers with your teacher, then suggest an alternative phrase for each of the expressions with *keep*.

1 The children kept _____ making a noise even though we had told them to be quiet.

2 That dog is really nasty. Make sure you keep _____ from him.

3 This fence should keep the cats _____ of the garden.

4 It's very difficult for the government to keep costs _____ .

5 We should really try to keep _____ with the neighbours.

6 We've got a very busy meeting so let's try and keep _____ the agenda.

3 Reporting verbs
(Language review 3, page 103)

Look at the tapescript for Exercise 1 on page 152. In which of the answerphone messages could you use the following reporting verbs: *suggest, apologise, warn, advise, remind, refuse*?

Now look at the two columns of sentences. Column 1 has sentences using *say* or *tell*. Column 2 has the same sentences with other reporting verbs.

1 What changes do you notice between each sentence in Column 1 and the corresponding sentence in Column 2?

2 Which of the reporting verbs in Column 2 are similar in the way we use them?

COLUMN 1

1 Mark said they should leave early.

2 The angry customer said he wouldn't pay the bill.

3 He said he was sorry for not going to the meeting.

4 She told us not to touch the plate as it was very hot.

5 James told us not to forget the meeting.

6 David's mother said it wasn't a good idea to watch so much T.V.

COLUMN 2

Mark suggested leaving early.

The angry customer refused to pay the bill.

He apologised for not going to the meeting.

She warned us not to touch the plate as it was very hot.

James reminded us not to forget the meeting.

She advised David not to watch so much T.V.

4 Practice

In pairs, look again at the tapescript for Exercise 1 on page 152. Take it in turns to put the messages to Paul into reported speech, making use of the reporting verbs in Exercise 3. Student B should write down the reported message.

EXAMPLE:

Jim Tate rang. He said his car was out of action again and it was with the mechanic. He advised Paul to go by bus the next day.

When you have finished, compare your five reported messages with another pair of students. Correct any mistakes that you find.

page 100 UNIT 11 Stage two

5 Making excuses

When Sarah phones Paul, she thanks him for the invitation, apologises for not accepting and makes an excuse:

'Many thanks for inviting us to lunch on Sunday but I'm afraid we won't be able to make it. My mother's coming over that day.'

1 Look at each of the pictures. In pairs, practise asking someone to do something or go somewhere. Student B should make up an outrageous excuse. The first one has been done for you.

1 A *Could you clean the car?*
  B *Sorry. I'm allergic to soap.*

2 Now change partners and report the excuses. Use the example to help you:

She said she couldn't clean the car because she was allergic to soap.

Choose what you think was the best excuse out of the six. Compare it with the best excuses chosen by the other pairs.

---

6 Listening

1 Listen to the conversation between Anne and Colin about their holiday preparations. What two things went wrong?

2 Now listen to the tape again and put A (Anne) or C (Colin) in the box next to each of the things they said they would do. Also write the appropriate verb for each item. The first one has been done for you.

<u>pick up</u> children's passports [C]   _____ medical insurance [A e C]
_____ car insurance [C]   _____ ferry tickets [ ]
_____ traveller's cheques [A]   _____ currency [A]
_____ food [A]   _____ suitcase [ ] ?

3 Use this information to make sentences about what Anne and Colin said they would do.

EXAMPLE:

Colin said he was going to arrange the medical insurance.
Colin told Anne he was going to arrange the medical insurance.

UNIT 11 Stage two   page 101

Activity

Criminals Overheard

1 Reading and speaking

Student A: Turn to page 143.

Student B: Read these instructions.

You are a police detective interviewing Student A who recently overheard two criminals in a pub. Get a good description of the criminals and ask for a full report of what the two men said.

You also have a report from a police informer which you can use. Give Student A the details of what the informer said.

```
        NOTES ON INFORMATION GIVEN BY MR X BY PHONE,
                    10.08 P.M., 16/2/91

Informer reported robbery planned for 3rd week in
March. Two, possibly three, men involved - one
definitely Mick Parsons, 33 years. Robbery probably
in North London - Hampstead or Golders Green. Men
going to use guns and try to get jewellery and
silver.
```

When you have exchanged information, show your partner the following pictures of suspects to try and identify the criminals.

Suspect A

Suspect B

Suspect C

Suspect D

Suspect E

Suspect F

2 Writing

Work in pairs.

Use all the information to write a report of what was said in both cases.

Language review

1 Direct speech

We use direct speech to report the actual words someone said. With direct speech we use reporting verbs, e.g. *said, told someone, shouted, whispered*:

'I'm innocent,' he shouted.
'A man is helping us with our enquiries,' a police spokesman told us.
'You can't smoke here,' she said.
'I told you,' he whispered.

Direct speech is very common in newspapers and books where it gives a dramatic effect and allows readers to interpret someone's words for themselves. We can easily recognise direct speech as the speaker's words are always used in inverted commas.

2 Reported speech

Notice the main differences between direct and reported speech:

'I'm very disappointed,' she said.
She said (that) she was very disappointed.

'A man is helping us,' a police spokesman said.
A police spokesman said (that) a man was helping them.

'I've never done anything dishonest,' he said.
He said (that) he had never done anything dishonest.

'I'll see you tomorrow,' she said.
She said (that) she would see me the next day.

Differences:

1 Verb tenses - further into the past: *will → would*.
2 Word order - *she said* comes first instead of last.
3 Pronouns - direct to indirect: *I → she, you → me*.
4 Time reference - *tomorrow → the next day*.

Notice that we are not concerned about reporting the exact words someone used but the *meaning* of what they said.

Some items do not change in reported speech:
1 gerunds (*going, doing* etc.)
2 infinitives (after *make, see*, etc.)
3 certain tenses which are already in the past and cannot be changed - e.g. Past Perfect (*had done*)

*'I really like **going** to the cinema,'* she said.
She said she really liked **going** to the cinema.

*'I saw her **arrive** with another student,'* he said.
He said he had seen her **arrive** with another student.

*'**She'd left** before we arrived,'* he said.
He told us **she'd left** before they arrived.

Remember that the past of *must* is *had to*:

'I must write to Terry,' she said.
She said she **had to** write to Terry.

Notice the following changes in time references:

DIRECT SPEECH	REPORTED SPEECH
tomorrow	the next/following day
this Friday	that Friday
yesterday	the previous day/the day before
today	that day
next week/month	the following week/month
before	previously/earlier
the day before yesterday	two days earlier/before
the day after tomorrow	in two days' time

3 Reporting verbs

Apart from *say* and *tell*, we can sometimes use other reporting verbs:

to advise, warn, apologise, remind, refuse etc.

Most of these verbs are followed by the infinitive:

She advised me to catch an earlier train.
They warned us not to swim too near the rocks.
He reminded them to confirm their return flight.
We refused to accept the decision.

But notice:

*Julian apologised for **missing** the rehearsal.*

*Jill suggested **going** for a walk.*
or
*Jill suggested (that) **they should go** for a walk.*

UNIT 12

Opener

◆ Look at the beginnings of some letters to the problem page of a magazine. Then match the photos of people with the letters.

A
I'm really embarrassed about my voice. I moved up to London from Cornwall and my accent seems to stand out a mile. All the other blokes at work tease me.

B
I'm 21 and living at home. My problem is my parents – they're driving me mad. I've just come back from the South where I worked for six months and was my own person.

C
I feel very lonely and unhappy. I find it impossible to make friends. I always seem to end up by myself at parties.

D
I can't bear the thought of Christmas coming up. I know it's supposed to be a happy time but no-one in the family does anything to help me.

◆ Discuss these points with a partner.

1 Why do people write to magazines?
2 What sort of things do they write about?

Stage one

People in Crisis

1 Pre-listening

Look at this extract from a photo-story and identify the problem.

She's too young

Oh Amy listen to me. I'm worried about you

I'm marrying him and that's that! Just leave me alone

I'm going round to Sharon's. I'm tired of arguing with you

2 Listening

1 Listen to the first conversation and answer the questions.

a How old is Amy?
b How is Anne feeling?
c What does her friend advise her to do?
d What does Anne say she'll do?

2 Now listen to the next conversation and answer the questions.

a How old is Amy's boyfriend?
b What information does Anne give about Amy's boyfriend?
c What does Nick advise her to do?
d How did Amy react when her mother tried to talk to her?
e What final advice does Nick give Anne?

3 Finally, answer these questions after listening to Anne's third conversation.

a Does Ella smoke?
b What does Ella say about Amy's attitude?
c Who do you think Paul is?
d What advice does Ella give Anne?
e What else is Anne going to do?

What advice would *you* give to Anne? In pairs note down a few pieces of advice and discuss them with other students.

UNIT 12 Stage one   page 105

3 Vocabulary

1 In pairs, define these words. Use a dictionary if you need help.

> fiancé(e) • steady girlfriend • father-in-law
> close friend • colleague • classmate • neighbour
> ex husband/wife • stepmother • single woman
> bachelor • best friend

2 Look at this list of expressions from Anne's conversations.

> get on • go out • be in love • get engaged
> get married • get divorced

Now complete each sentence using the most suitable expression from the list. Use the correct form of the verbs.

1 Sharon and Clive have been _____ together for over three years.
2 Unfortunately Joseph doesn't _____ with his boss.
3 Jim and Katey _____ last week! The wedding's in March.
4 In Britain one in three married couples _____ .
5 Susan is _____ at St. Mary's church next weekend.
6 The film's about a university student who _____ with one of her teachers.

4 Asking for and giving advice
(Language review 1, page 113)

In pairs, look at the tapescript for Exercise 2 on page 152. Make a list of all the phrases which ask for advice, give advice or show a need for advice. Compare your list with another pair of students.

EXAMPLES:

What on earth am I going to do?	(asking for advice)
You should have a long talk with her.	(giving advice)
I really need to talk to you.	(showing a need for advice)

5 Reading and discussion

Read these longer extracts from the readers' letters on page 104.

Find words or phrases in the letters which mean the same as the following:

1 to be very noticeable (extract A)
2 make fun of (extract A)
3 an ignorant country person (extract A)
4 regular (extract B)
5 invent (extract C)
6 complaining (extract D)

Now, in groups of three, discuss what advice you would give in each case and why. Then compare your ideas with another group and decide which advice you think is best.

A I'm really embarrassed about my voice. I moved up to London from Cornwall and my accent seems to stand out a mile. All the other blokes at work tease me. I've been offered a promotion but it's really getting me down. All my mates have girlfriends but I haven't asked any girls out in case they think I'm a country bumpkin or something.

B I'm 21 and living at home. My problem is my parents – they're driving me mad. I've just come back from the South where I worked for six months and was my own person. Now I'm back they've returned to the same old routine – 'Where are you going?' and 'When will you be back?' I've got a steady boyfriend and we're thinking of getting engaged, but they still think I'm a child.

C I feel lonely and unhappy. I find it impossible to make friends. I always seem to end up by myself at parties. People seem to like me at first but after a while they stop phoning and they make up reasons for not seeing me. I thought things would improve as I got older but I'm 34 now.

D I can't bear the thought of Christmas coming up. I know it's supposed to be a happy time but no-one in the family does anything to help me. I do all the cooking and washing-up while everyone just sits around. If I complain, the kids say I'm nagging and my husband goes out for a walk with the dog.

6 Pronunciation

1 Listen to the words on the tape and practise saying them.

2 You are now going to hear eight sentences which contain the eight words below. Listen and decide whether the words are pronounced with /ʊ/ or /ɔː/. Put them into two groups.

1 thought	4 Paul	7 walk
2 would	5 talk	8 cooking
3 should	6 good	

3 Choose the vowel sound that doesn't match in each case.

1 forced   bored   saw   first   lawn
2 pull   look   pool   shook   foot
3 word   learn   third   door
4 food   full   grew   loose

7 Practice
(Language review 1, page 112)

Read this reply to letter A.

There is quite a lot of 'direct' advice in this letter. Underline all the examples you can find.

Susan Soames advises...

Dear ...,
What a shame the way you talk is causing you such distress. It's unfortunately true that people are often very arrogant and insulting about others who speak differently. But I certainly don't think you should give up your job because of it. Your employers aren't worried about the way you speak, are they? Why don't you talk to girls? I'm sure you'll find loads of them who love your accent. Stand up for yourself! Ignore or hit back (verbally) at people who take the mickey out of you. Your accent means you've always got something to talk about, so take advantage of it!
Yours sincerely,
Susan

● **Vocabulary**

Choose the best meaning for the following words and phrases from the letter.

1 distress	a unhappiness	b anger	c amusement
2 insulting	a caring	b rude	c bored
3 give up	a leave	b apply for	c stay in
4 loads	a a few	b some	c lots
5 stand up for yourself	a give up	b fight back	c go away
6 take the mickey	a attack	b understand	c make fun of

● **Writing**

Write a similar letter of reply to one of the other letters on page 106. Read your reply to your partner and compare the different advice you have given.

8 Game

- Write a letter to a magazine about a real or imaginary problem.
- Give your letter to your teacher, who will then give you a different one.
- Guess who in the class wrote the letter and write a reply.

- Identify your letter and tell the class whether the reply was addressed to the right person.
- Finally, grade the reply you received using the following scale.

  Understanding of the problem: 10 points
  Tone of the letter: 10 points
  Usefulness of advice: 10 points
  Maximum possible total = 30 points

Stage two

Worries and Concerns

1 Pre-reading

In groups of three, make a list of ten things which can go wrong while you are on holiday.

2 Reading

Look at the headline of the newspaper article and put the words into the right order.

Now read the article and put the three separate paragraphs (A, B and C) into a suitable position in the text.

How many of the things you mentioned in Exercise 1 are also referred to in the article?

> ## We're to have on just holiday too fun worried
>
> By Willy Newlands Travel Correspondent
>
> 1 Most Britons take their troubles with them on holiday, according to a new survey.
> 2 Although 40 per cent said the main reason for going away is to escape stress, almost all said they worry more than they do at home. Only four in every 100 are carefree and happy.
> 3 ****
> 4 More than a quarter fear they will be upset by rowdy holidaymakers and 22 per cent have nightmares about being mugged.
> 5 ****
> 6 More cheerfully, one in seven of the sample – including 10 per cent of pensioners – say their idea of a good holiday is 'sun, sea and nightlife.'
> 7 ****
> 8 The research also showed that the traditional stay-at-home Briton is no more. Three out of every five adults now want to holiday abroad, a marked increase from the figures only three years ago. Then less than half wanted to go overseas.
> 9 The hotel holiday is still a winner, with just over half of all Britons interviewed preferring being cosseted to going on a self-catering holiday, despite worries about cheeky waiters and rowdy fellow guests.

A A quarter of all young, single, men found this to be the most attractive formula for a holiday, according to the MORI survey, conducted for GIS Leisure-care.

B The most common concern is burglary, with four out of 10 fretting about their homes being broken into while they're abroad.

C One in five think the car may break down, and the same number are upset about the chances of bad weather.

● **Reading for detail**

Answer the following questions. You will only have to read parts of the article to find the correct answers.

1 How many people in the survey worry more on holiday than when they are at home?
2 What is the second most common concern of holidaymakers?
3 Which group prefers 'sun, sea and nightlife' on their holiday?
4 Why are hotel holidays so popular?

Underline all the words and phrases in the article which are used to express worry and concern.

EXAMPLE: … 'they worry more than they do at home.'

3 Vocabulary

Choose the best meaning for each of these words from the article.

1 carefree (para. 2)	a concerned	b relaxed	c busy
2 fretting (para. 3)	a complaining	b worrying	c laughing
3 rowdy (para. 4)	a unfriendly	b noisy	c polite
4 mugged (para. 4)	a attacked & robbed	b cheated	c kidnapped

Find words which mean the same as the following:

5 people interviewed (para. 6) — *the sample*
6 retired people (para. 6)
7 recipe (para. 7) — *formula*
8 carried out (para. 7) — *conducted*
9 notable (para. 8) — *marked*
10 looked after (para. 9) — *cosseted*

page 108 | UNIT 12

● **Statistics**

Write down all the expressions in the article which express statistics.

EXAMPLES: *40 per cent*
almost all

Now classify them in order of the greatest to the smallest number.

4 Question forming and interview

1 What were the questions asked in the survey which produced the information in the article? In pairs, write down five questions you think fit the results of the survey.

EXAMPLE: *What is your main reason for going away on holiday?*

2 When you have completed your list of questions, use them to interview three other people to find out why they go on holiday, what worries them while they are away and what kind of holiday they prefer. How similar are the results to the ones in the article?

5 Pre-reading

What do you understand by the word *stress*? Look at the causes of stress listed below. In pairs, put them in order, numbering the most stressful 1 and least stressful 10.

Losing a job ☐
Holiday ☐
Divorce ☐
Retirement ☐
Change in sleeping habits ☐

Leaving school ☐
Change in living conditions ☐
Change in responsibilities at work ☐
Personal injury or illness ☐
Change in eating habits ☐

UNIT 12 Stage two   page **109**

6 Reading

Now read this article on stress. Why does stress sometimes cause illness?

Stress

In a stressful world which is full of change, most of us have to cope with the problems of growing up, going to school, forming relationships, having children, making a home, holding down a job, bereavement, problems with children, illness and much more besides. Many of these problems are in no way 'our fault', yet they can often have a profound effect on our health, often reducing our ability to withstand infections and even making us susceptible to killer diseases such as cancer. Several studies have confirmed that stress impairs the functioning of the immune system.

The typical responses of individuals to bad luck and stress vary enormously. A few people seem to enjoy overcoming problems but it is probably true to say that more 'illness' and 'disease' is caused by stressful events in people's lives than by 'real' disease. But as well as these 'external' causes of stress and emotional upheaval, there are many more 'internal' or self-generated causes and some people are more likely to be troubled with these than are others. Beliefs or personality types are examples of these.

Decide whether the following statements are true or false, according to the text. Circle the letter T or F.

1 Many problems in life can influence our health.   T/F
2 Stress produces serious diseases like cancer.   T/F
3 Everyone has the a similar reaction to stress.   T/F
4 Stress is a major cause of health problems.   T/F
5 The type of character a person has can cause stress.   T/F

7 Listening

Listen to this interview in groups of three and note down your answers to the following questions.

Student A What are the main causes of stress?
Student B What are the main symptoms stress produces?
Student C What are the three main ways of dealing with stress?

Now listen to the interview again and together check all the information you noted down. Make any necessary corrections.

8 The First Conditional
(Language review 2, page 113)

In the recorded interview the doctor says *'If someone has to rush to the office every day, works under a lot of pressure ..., that person will probably suffer from some kind of stress.'*

Look at the tapescript for Exercise 7 on page 153 and underline all the other *if* clauses. Try to decide:
(a) how we form this tense
(b) what other words we can use with the First Conditional instead of *will*
(c) what difference these words make to the meaning.

Finally, look at the example from the tapescript which begins with *Unless*. What do you think is the difference between *unless* and *if* in the First Conditional?

9 Superlative adjectives
(Language review 3, page 113)

In the results of the holiday survey, the newspaper article on page 108 says

'A quarter of all young, single men found this to be the most attractive formula for a holiday ...'

'The biggest concern is burglary.'

These are both examples of superlatives. Look at the tapescript for Exercise 7 on page 153 and write down any other examples of superlatives you can find. Then try to decide when we use *the* + adjective + *est*, as in *'the biggest concern'* and when we use *the* + *most* + adjective, as in *'the most attractive formula'*.

10 Pronunciation

Read these sentences and see if you can identify the stressed words.

EXAMPLE: *That house is the most attractive one in the street.*

1 Insomnia, poor appetite and a feeling of tiredness are some of the most common symptoms of stress.
2 Sometimes the smallest things can be stress-related.
3 People's biggest concern while they are on holiday is burglary.
4 The best type of holiday for many people is in a hotel.
5 A hotel is usually the most expensive type of accommodation.
6 The weather is often the most important factor for a holiday.

Now listen to the same sentences on the tape and check your answers.

11 Practice

● The First Conditional

The doctor in the interview says:

'If someone doesn't get any exercise and worries a lot as well, they can easily become stressed.'

We could also say:

Unless people get some exercise and worry less, they will/might/can easily become stressed.

Match the descriptions of people (1–4) with the four photographs and talk about future possibilities in the same way.

1 ... smokes 40 cigarettes a day, drives to work and has an important job in a large bank.
2 ... is overweight, doesn't do any exercise and eats too many cakes, biscuits and sweets.
3 ... worries about school and exams, never goes out and watches T.V. every night.
4 ... works 10 hours a day, takes work home in the evenings and at weekends, suffers from insomnia and can't relax.

Steve   Diane   Brian   Janet

● Superlatives

Complete the following questions with the correct form and discuss them. Then choose the most suitable answer for each question from the list below.

EXAMPLE:

What is the world's (long) railway line?
What is the world's longest railway line? The Trans-Siberian.

> The Vatican City • Jupiter • 1903
> Mandarin Chinese • Caspian Sea • The Mona Lisa
> Hawaii • Anthony and Cleopatra
> Chile • Trans-Siberian

1 Where is the (wet) place in the world?
2 What was the (valuable) object ever stolen?
3 Which country has had the (bad) earthquake?
4 Which was the (expensive) film ever made?
5 Which is the (big) planet in the Solar System?
6 What is the (common) language spoken today?
7 Which is the (small) independent country in the world?
8 When was the (early) flight by man?
9 Which is the world's (large) lake?

UNIT 12 Stage two   page 111

Activity

A Helping Hand

1 Reading

Look at the text and say where you might find it and what you think it is about.

> **6.15 Helping Hand.** A chance for listeners with different problems to phone in and ask for help and advice from a panel of experts. Introduced by Penny Cowdrey.

2 Listening

Work in groups of three.

Listen to these extracts from a radio phone-in programme and after each one complete the profile details.

	Age	Problem
Caller 1		
Caller 2		
Caller 3		

3 Discussion

In the same groups as a panel, discuss each caller's problem and give your opinions and advice. When you have finished, exchange your ideas with another group.

4 Writing

Imagine you are an 'agony aunt' working for the problem page of a magazine. Write to one of the callers as if they had written to you. Advise the person what to do, basing your advice on the discussion you had in your group.

Language review

1 Advice

● Should
Should is used to ask for and give advice:

What should I do?
You should have a long talk with her.

● If I were you ...
This expression is often used to give advice:

If I were you, I'd ring the boyfriend's parents.
or
I'd ring the boyfriend's parents if I were you. (no comma)

Notice we often omit *if I were you* in conversation:

I'd ring the boyfriend's parents. (if I were you)
I would try to be patient. (if I were you)

Notice also:

What would you do? (if you were me)

● Why don't you ...?
We also use this question to give advice:

Why don't you talk to both of them?

● Imperatives
Although we use imperatives to give orders and instructions, they are also used to give direct advice, especially between friends or when we are trying to encourage someone:

Come on! Don't worry. Give Sharon a ring.
Try not to be too hard on yourself.

2 The First Conditional

● Form
if + Present Simple followed by *will/can/might* + infinitive.
(Do NOT use *will, can* or *might* with the *if* clause.)

We use the First Conditional to talk about possibilities in the future:

If you continue to smoke so many cigarettes, you'll get ill.
If you don't eat well, you can get ill more easily.
If you don't try to relax more, you might suffer from stress.

If we reverse the order, the meaning does not change but we omit the comma:

You'll get ill if you continue to smoke so many cigarettes.

Will expresses a more definite possibility than *can*, and *might* suggests an even less likely possibility.

Unless and *until* can replace *if + not*:

Unless/until we realise the effects of stress, we won't do anything about it.

When is also used in the First Conditional when we are sure something is going to happen:

When the car is serviced it won't lose so much oil.
or
The car won't lose so much oil when it's serviced.

3 Superlative adjectives

Notice the different types of superlative adjectives.

a Regular: adjective + *est*:
   high highest, large largest, hard hardest

b Where the adjective changes its spelling:
   big biggest (adjectives spelt with consonant + vowel + consonant double the final consonant)
   thin thinnest, hot hottest
   lovely loveliest (*y* endings become *iest*)
   ugly ugliest, tiny tiniest

c Irregular superlatives: *best, worst*
   That's the best film I've seen for ages.
   The company had its worst results for five years.

Normally we use *-est* for shorter adjectives and *most* for longer ones:

He's one of the richest men in the world.
That was the most uncomfortable journey I've ever been on.

We always use *most* for adjectives ending in *-ing* or *-ous*:

This is the most boring book I've read for a long time.
Lawrence Olivier was one of the most famous English actors.

Sometimes we can use either form. In these cases *the most* is used to give more emphasis:

The commonest place for accidents is in the home.
The most common place for accidents is in the home.

UNIT 12 Language review

UNIT 13

Opener

- What sports do you play? Have you ever been injured while you were playing a game?
- Look at these photographs and pick out the three most dangerous sports. What makes them dangerous?

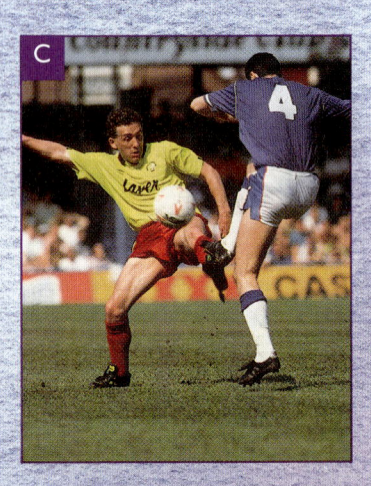

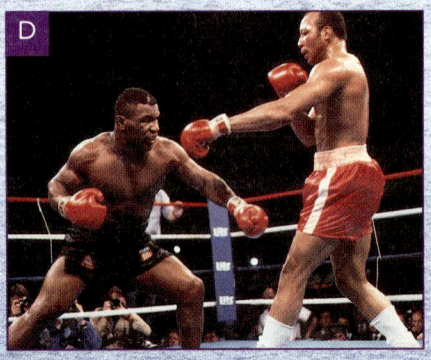

- Compare your three most dangerous sports with your partner's.

Stage one

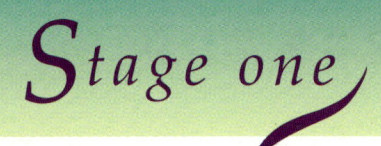

Dangers and Uncertainties

1 Listening

Listen to these five conversations and match each one with one of the topics A-H.

A holiday plans ☐ 3
B job dissatisfaction ☐ 4
C weather ☐
D an invitation to a sports event ☐ 1
E buying a new car ☐
F travel plans ☐ 2
G buying new clothes ☐ 5
H marriage problems ☐

2 Evidence

Listen to the conversations again and make a note of the words or phrases which helped you to decide what each one was about. Fill in a table like this:

	Subject	Words and phrases
1	sporting event	game, played, scored 5 goals
2		

Now discuss possible answers to these questions with your partner. Look at the tapescript on page 154 if you need to.

a Why does Simon think that it will be 'a good game'? (1)
b Why does Jane want to fly? (2)
c How do you know that Liz and John have already been to North Africa? (3)
d How do you know that Dave has been to university before? (4)
e Who do you think Tony is? (5)
f What do you think Maria is going to buy? (5)

3 Vocabulary

● **Informal words and expressions**

Match these informal words and phrases from the conversations with the more formal 'translations':

1 to make up your mind
2 come on
3 to give someone a ring
4 ages
5 who knows?
6 fed up
7 a chat
8 it didn't do any good

a a very long time
b an informal conversation
c unhappy/miserable
d I don't know
e to decide
f the situation got no better
g to telephone someone
h you must/should come

○ **Useful verbs: *have* and *feel***

Look at the tapescript for Exercise 1 on page 154 again and find ...

a two expressions which include the verb *have*.
b two expressions which include the verb *feel*.

What other expressions do you know using these two verbs?

Have	Feel
to have a bath	to feel happy

4 Certainty and uncertainty

(Language review 1 and 3, page 122)

Here are some of the expressions used by the speakers in the five conversations. Decide whether the expressions show that the speaker is certain or uncertain about something in the future.

1 I might (come to the match).
2 I haven't made up my mind yet.
3 It'll take us at least two days.
4 We might crash. I might be sick.
5 You'll certainly feel sick.
6 We may go to North Africa again.
7 I thought I might go somewhere on my own.
8 I'm definitely going to resign.
9 I'll probably have a holiday.
10 I may apply for something abroad.
11 Tony might think it's too short.
12 Maybe I'll buy this one instead.

Look again at the expressions with *will* and *going to*. Which words show that the speaker is uncertain? Which words show that the speaker is certain?

Look at all the other 'uncertain' expressions. Which words show the speakers' uncertainty?

UNIT 13 Stage one   page 115

5 Pronunciation

The stresses in English sentences are on words which give new or important information.

Listen to and repeat these five sentences from the conversations in Exercise 1. Listen again and decide which is the new or important information.

The words or parts of words (syllables) without stresses are weak. They are spoken more quickly. This mixture of stressed and unstressed syllables gives English its rhythm.

Now read these sentences aloud with a partner. Stress the information which you think is new or important.

1 I spent all weekend in bed.
2 I was sure I was going to die.
3 I've never felt so ill in my life.
4 On Sunday morning I decided to phone the doctor.
5 He gave me some pills and told me to stay off work.

Now listen to the recording. Did you stress the same words as the speaker on the tape?

6 Weekend plans survey
(Language review 1 and 3, page 122)

Work in groups of four. Ask about people's plans for next weekend.

EXAMPLE: *What are you going to do on Saturday morning?*

Answer the questions like this:

I'm going to play football. (if you are certain)
I may/might play football. (if you are uncertain)

Fill in the details in a group diary, like this:

	Saturday Morning Afternoon Evening	Sunday Morning Afternoon Evening
Student A		

7 Worries

With a partner, look at the people in the pictures. They are all worrying about something. What do you think they are saying to themselves?

Make a list of their worries.

EXAMPLE:

1 'They might want to search my case. I might miss my connecting flight.'

8 Role play

Work in pairs.

Student A: Turn to page 143.

Student B: Read the following instructions.

You are a pessimist. You always think things are going to go wrong. When your partner tells you some of his/her ambitions, point out to him/her some of the bad things that might happen.

EXAMPLE:

A *I want to walk across the Sahara Desert.*
B *I don't think you should. You might get lost and die of thirst.*

If your partner argues, think of something else that might go wrong.

Stage two

Possibilities

1 Reading

Look at these three photographs. What do you think they show? Exchange ideas with a partner.

Now check your ideas by reading the text on the next page.

Riddle of the Rings

Mysterious circles have suddenly appeared in cornfields all over the world. They've been seen in Japan, France and Brazil, but southern England has the most.

Experts have put forward many theories to explain the circles, but no-one has ever seen them being made. They could be the result of whirlwinds, or freak storms; some people have even suggested that they could be marks left by animals.

A professor from Glasgow University has said: 'It's a very interesting mystery, but none of the explanations seems to fit.' Of course, we'd all like to believe that the rings could be marks left after little green men have landed their spaceships. But scientists have rejected this idea. They say that UFOs could not be the cause, because not all the circles are round. The theories involving animals, like hedgehogs or deer, seem unlikely because no-one has been any animals behaving strangely.

And of course, whenever there is a mystery like this, there are cynics who say that the circles could be the work of jokers. The most likely explanation is the weather. Most experts believe the whirlwind theory is the winner. They think that strong, spiralling winds may flatten the corn in the fields.

In the end we have to decide for ourselves. We may never know the true answer, unless, of course, someone actually sees the little green men.

● Understanding

What suggestions have been made to explain the circles. Read the text again carefully and complete a table like this:

Which theory do the experts think is the most probable?

Explanation/Theory	Why this theory is improbable
1	
2	

2 Vocabulary

Scan the text again and find:

1 two words which mean people who know a lot about a subject
2 two words (nouns) for the shapes in the fields
3 two words for types of violent weather
4 the names of two kinds of animals
5 a word which means to suggest (an idea)

● Verbs ending in -en

Some adjectives can be made into verbs by adding -en.

EXAMPLE: *Strong spiralling winds may flatten the corn in the fields.*

to flatten = to make (something) flat

Fill the gaps in these sentences with verbs ending in -en

1 The road through the village is too narrow. They're going to _____ it.

2 I can't write with this pencil; it's too blunt. I must _____ it.

3 The trousers I've just bought are too long, so I'm going to _____ them.

4 If the butter's too hard, you can _____ it by putting it somewhere warm.

5 Soldiers who go out on patrol at night sometimes _____ their faces with charcoal.

3 Most

(Language review 4, page 122)

Scan the text for sentences which contain the word *most*. How many different uses of *most* are there? Compare ideas with a partner.

Without changing their meaning, rewrite the sentences replacing the word *most*.

4 Possibilities: could, may, might
(Language review 1 and 2, page 122)

In Exercise 1 you listed possible theories for how the circles in the fields were made.

With a partner suggest some possible explanations for the mysteries in the photographs. Use 'possibility' expressions like those in the text.

5 Magazine stories

Which of these magazine stories would you choose to read? What could the story be about? What do the title and the summary tell you?

Discuss your ideas with your partner, then make up a possible storyline for the story you have chosen.

Lee Taylor's enchanting Victorian romance continues.

In Lilac Time

Suddenly it occurred to Laura that she knew nothing about her fascinating employer - not even if he had a wife.

Seeing, Believing

Neil was an observer; that was his great gift ... he could see things as they really were.

Only Yesterday
by Jan Mazzoni

It was all she'd always wanted - a room by the sea, a life far away and time to be alone. But still she couldn't forget.

UNIT 13 Stage two   page 119

6 Writing: mini-sagas

A mini-saga is a story with exactly 50 words. Read this example:

> ### A Life of Luxury
>
> Henry lives a life of luxury. He never works and spends most of his time asleep. A kind lady gets his meals, cleans the house and does the washing-up. Soon after she goes to bed, Henry goes out for the night. What he enjoys most is catching …

Guess the ending: there are three more words. (Check your guess by looking on page143.)

Write a mini-saga of your own. Make up a title or use one of these:

- The camera never lies
- I saw Elvis
- The Wall
- Just one cup of coffee
- On the move
- Moscow dream

Write the last three or four words on a separate piece of paper.

Exchange stories with a partner and guess the ending to your partner' story.

Activity

Soap Opera

1 Discussion
Work in groups of three or four.

Look at these pictures. What have they got in common?

What makes a good continuing serial – a soap opera? Write a list of the three most important features.

What is the most popular 'soap' in your country? Why do people love it or hate it?

2 Listening

Listen to these five people talking about their favourite soap operas. Do any of the speakers mention the reasons on your list?

3 Class survey: What makes a successful soap opera?

Ask other people in your class questions to find out what they would like in a new soap opera. Ask about:

1 the setting (e.g. Texas/London)
2 the characters (e.g. a local community/a rich family/business people)
3 the style (e.g. humorous/light/serious)

4 Brainstorming and writing
Work in groups of three.

You are going to write Episode One of a new soap opera. Base your ideas on the class survey.

Make quick decisions about the setting, the characters, and the style.

Take it in turns to develop a storyline.

EXAMPLE:

Student A *The story starts in Jane Blond's New York apartment. Jane comes in late one night and finds the window open.*

Student B *She is closing the window when she sees a man standing in the street. He's pointing something towards her. It might be a gun …*

Student C *… or it could be a camera – Jane isn't sure.*

Continue the story until you have agreed on the storyline for Scene 1. Write the storyline for Scene 1, before you go on to Scene 2.

When you have written three scenes, exchange stories with another group.

Think of a title for the soap opera given to your group.

UNIT 13 Activity   page 121

Language review

1 May and might

● Form

The form of *may* and *might* is the same for all persons:

I may / might
He may / might
We may / might
etc.

May and *might* are followed by an infinitive without *to*:

*I may **go** tomorrow.*
*They might **visit** their sister.*

● Use

We use *may* or *might* to talk about present possibilities:

I don't know where John is. He may / might be in the kitchen.

and to talk about future possibilities:

I may / might go to Spain for my holidays. I haven't decided yet.

● May or might?

There is not much difference in meaning between *may* and *might*. But if we think that something is very possible, we prefer *may*:

I may apply for something abroad.

If we think that something is improbable, or we have not really thought about it much, we prefer *might*:

I might come to the match. I haven't made up my mind yet.

2 Could

- Like *may* and *might*, we use *could* to talk about present or future possibilities:

  It could be cold outside. You'd better wear a coat.
  They could arrive any minute.
  He could still be waiting at the station.

Like *might*, *could* expresses less probability than *may*.

- Notice this difference in meaning between the negative forms of *may*, *might* and *could*:

  I may / might not come.
  = It's possible that I will not come.

  I couldn't come.
  = It wasn't possible for me to come. (Past)
  or It wouldn't be possible for me to come. (Future)

- Remember these other uses of *could*:

1 Suggestions:
   We could go to the theatre tonight.

2 Abilities (past of *can*):
   I could ride a bicycle when I was six years old.

3 Polite requests:
   Could I have two coffees, please?

3 How possible, how certain?

Here are some more ways of expressing possibility or (un)certainty:

I'll definitely see you on Friday.
(This is certain)

I'll probably go to the party.
(This is almost certain)

I'm likely to be late home tonight.
(This is probable)

I may / might see you on Friday.
Perhaps* I'll see you tomorrow.
Maybe* I'll see you next week.
(This is not certain, but it is possible)

We're unlikely to see Liz this week.
We probably* won't see Liz this week
(This is improbable)

I definitely* won't go back there.
(It is certain I won't)

*Notice the position of *perhaps, maybe, probably* and *definitely* in these sentences.

4 Most

Most means the majority of, the largest part of, or nearly all.

- Use *most* with uncountable nouns and plural countable nouns:

  Most fresh food is good for you.
  Most scientists do not believe in UFOs.

- Compare these two sentences:

  Most scientists do not believe in UFOs. (= the majority of all scientists)
  Most of the scientists I have met believe in UFOs.

- Use *the most* as a pronoun:

  There have been a lot of storms in France, Holland and Germany, but Britain has had the most. (= more storms than anywhere else).

Remember that *the most* is used to make superlative adjectives:

He's the most interesting speaker I have ever heard.

UNIT 14

Opener

◆ Describe each of the people in the cartoon who are asking for money.

◆ What do you think *'broke'* means?
What makes people beg for money in the streets?
Would it make any difference if society helped these people more?

◆ Do you give money to people in the street? Why or why not?
Discuss in pairs or groups.

Stage one

Wishful Thinking

1 Pre-listening

You are going to listen to three of these people talking about their economic situations.

Karl

Annie

Gary

Eileen

Look at the photographs and the list of words. Put a tick by the words you think you might hear on the tape.

job	defendant	boring
fiancé	neighbourhood	earn
stress	interesting	abroad
unemployed	money	polluted
salary	afford	stubborn
degree	flat	advise
training	company	

Rosa

Ken

2 Listening

Listen to the tape and check how many of the words in Exercise 1 you predicted correctly. At the same time, try to identify which three people in the photographs are talking about themselves.
Finally, match their names with the three kinds of jobs.

shop work   public transport
finance

3 Listening for detail

Listen to the tape again and complete the table. Compare your results with a partner.

Name			
Education			
Time in job		Since she left college	
Type of home			3-bedroomed semi
Opinion of Job	Badly paid, boring & tiring		
Hopes/ambitions			To go on a cruise

page 124 UNIT 14 Stage one

4 Vocabulary

Match the following words and phrases from the tape with the most suitable meaning. Refer to the tapescript on page 154 if you need to.

1 out of work   a not married
2 a plumber   b an academic qualification
3 make ends meet   c over-optimism
4 a degree   d a long boat journey for pleasure
5 abroad   e unemployed
6 single   f in/to a foreign country
7 a cruise   g have enough money for basic expenses
8 wishful thinking   h person who repairs water pipes, heating systems etc.

● **Money expressions**

In this unit you have met two expressions which refer to not having enough money: *to be broke* and *to make ends meet*.

What other expressions do you know for having too little or a lot of money?

Underline the 'money' expressions in these sentences and say whether they refer to having a lot, very little or no money.

1 She must be loaded. Look at that car!
2 I'm skint. Lend me a fiver, will you?
3 Thank goodness we're getting paid today. I'm a bit short at the moment.
4 After he sold his house he was very well off.
5 A lot of jobless people are living on the breadline.
6 They haven't got two pennies to rub together.
7 The Forsythes are rolling in money.
8 Fred and Joan have always been hard up.

5 The Second Conditional
(Language review 1, page 131)

Look at these five Second Conditional sentences:

1 If I had the time and money, I might do some sort of training course.
2 If I could afford it, I'd buy Margaret a watch.
3 If I had to be careful about how much I spent, I don't know what I would do.
4 I might consider getting married if I met the right kind of guy.
5 If I had a bit more money, I wouldn't complain.

Now look at these five First Conditional sentences:

6 If she works really hard, she'll probably pass the exam.
7 If you eat all that cake, you'll feel sick.
8 I'll ring you later if I have time.
9 I'll work abroad if I get the chance.
10 If we save enough money, we'll go on a cruise.

How are the two groups different? Think about (a) the words used and (b) the meaning of the sentences.

6 Practice

Gary mentions that his flat is not in very good condition and that the neighbourhood is a bit run down. Some possible problems of deprived areas are given in the table.

Work in pairs, and for each problem, write a possible solution as in the example. When you have finished, compare your answers with another pair of students.

PROBLEM	POSSIBLE SOLUTION
1 Buildings in terrible condition	If the local people helped to do up the buildings, it would help to improve things.
2 Vandalism	
3 No parks, gardens or play areas for children	
4 Old people who are lonely and/or ill	
5 Shops and cinemas a long way from where people live	

7 Personalised practice

Look again at the information in Exercise 3 about people's lives and how they would like them to be different.

For each of the headings opposite, write down the changes you would like to make in your *own* life. Then tell your partner about these changes.

EXAMPLES: *I'd like to buy a flat if I had enough money.*
If I had time, I'd like to learn another language.

Make a note of your partner's changes.

	You	Your partner
Work/university/school		
House/home		
Personal relationships		
Ambitions/hopes for the future		
Courses/training		
Travel		

8 Writing

Using the information about your partner, write a report of the main changes he/she would like to make in those areas.

Stage two

Recommendations

1 Pre-reading

Can you identify this country? With a partner write down five things you know about the country and five differences between this country and the country you are in.

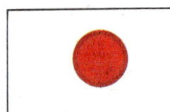

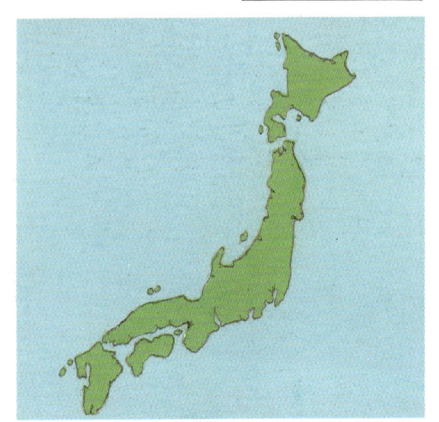

page 126   UNIT 14   Stage two

2 Reading

Read this text and say where you think it comes from.

Visiting Japan

Japan is an unusual mixture of traditional and ultra-modern. This can be confusing for the visitor because, although it looks quite western, Japan is still in many ways very oriental. Whenever you go into a house you must take off your shoes. Sometimes your host will provide you with slippers, if not you walk round in your socks. A visitor should also expect in more traditional houses, hotels and restaurants to eat kneeling down on the floor on a cushion in front of a low table. It's a good idea to get used to eating with chopsticks but, if you can't manage, ask for a knife and fork. The Japanese are extremely polite and hospitable: you can nearly always find someone who speaks English. In summer the country is very hot and humid so anyone planning a trip then ought to take light, comfortable clothes with them.

The majority of tourists head for Tokyo but you ought not to miss the chance of visiting the old capital cities of Kyoto and Nara. From Tokyo you can get to Kyoto in 3 hours on the 'Shinkansen' super-express. If you are driving it's important to remember that in Japan you have to drive on the left-hand side of the road. To get round the sights you can hire a bicycle for 250 yen an hour. (US$1.00 = 180 yen.)

For a change from western-style hotels you ought to try one of the traditional inns, 'Ryokan'. Instead of a bed you'll sleep on the floor on a 'futon' mattress and cover spread over the 'tatami' floor mat. To relax at the end of a hard day's touring you should enjoy a long soak in the 'ofuro' – the traditional Japanese hot bath prior to sampling a delicious Japanese meal.

Which of the following topics are mentioned in the text? Put a tick by the ones you think are included.

history ☐   festivals ☐   transport ☐
food ☐   sport ☐   customs ☐   art ☐
accommodation ☐   climate ☐   language ☐

UNIT 14 Stage two   page 127

● **Understanding**

To answer the following questions you do not have to read the whole text. First find which part of the article has the information you need, then answer the question.

1 What is the traditional Japanese way to sit for a meal?
2 How important is it for a visitor to speak some Japanese?
3 What is unusual about driving in Japan?
4 How is a 'futon' different from a normal bed?

According to the text, are the following statements true or false? Put a circle round the letter T or F.

5 It's normal to take your shoes off when going into a Japanese house. T/F
6 You have to use chopsticks in Japan. T/F
7 Japanese summers are warm and dry. T/F
8 Kyoto used to be the capital of Japan. T/F
9 It costs over US$2.00 an hour to hire a bike. T/F
10 A 'tatami' is a kind of chair. T/F

3 Vocabulary

Read the text again and find:

1 two time expressions which refer to frequency.
2 a word which means the same as *very*.
3 a word which means the same as *give*.
4 a word which means the opposite of *unfriendly*.
5 a word which means *places to see*.
6 a word which means the same as *before*.

● **Adjectives with -able**

Some adjectives can be formed by adding the suffix *-able* to a verb or noun.
EXAMPLES: comfort - comfortable   love - lovable

Complete these sentences with adjectives ending in *-able*. Use the noun or verb at the end of the sentence to help you.

1 The lunch after the meeting was a most _____ one. AGREE
2 John won't mind sleeping on the floor. He's very _____. ADAPT
3 Thank goodness this coat is _____. It's terribly dirty. WASH
4 Alex is feeling a bit _____. He's just had a vaccination. IRRITATE
5 Doesn't Philip look _____. What's the matter with him? MISERY
6 That painting must be really _____. It's by Van Gogh. VALUE
7 I really want to see that film. It got very _____ reviews. FAVOUR
8 Short hair is very _____ at the moment. FASHION

4 Recommendations and obligations
(Language review 2, page 131)

In the text about Japan there are several examples of language used to express recommendations or obligations:

Whenever you go to a house you must take off your shoes. (obligation)

… you ought not to miss the chance of visiting the old capital cities of Kyoto and Nara. (recommendation)

Scan the text and make a list of sentences which make recommendations or express obligations. Discuss your ideas with a partner.

5 Articles
(Language review 3, page 131)

Look at the following sentences from the text about Japan and try to decide why the definite or indefinite article is used.

1 Whenever you go into a house you must take off your shoes.
2 A visitor should also expect … to eat kneeling down on the floor … in front of a low table.
3 The Japanese are extremely polite and hospitable.
4 In summer the country is very hot and humid.
5 From Tokyo you can get to Kyoto in 3 hours on the 'Shinkansen' super-express.
6 Instead of a bed you'll sleep on the floor on a 'futon' mattress.

6 Pronunciation

Look at the following sentences and decide which words are contracted in normal speech. The first one has been done for you.

Underline the words you would contract, then practise saying the contractions with a partner.

1 If you eat all that cake, you will feel sick.
   If you eat all that cake, you'll feel sick.
2 You should not miss the chance to try sushi.
3 If you are driving in Britain, it is necessary to drive on the left.
4 If you are travelling by plane, it is not a good idea to eat to much.
5 If he comes early, we will go to the cinema.
6 I would go to Hawaii if I had enough money.
7 I would not lose my temper if I were you.

Now listen to the tape and check your answers.

---

7 Practice

Work in pairs.

Student A: Read this advice for visitors to Saudi Arabia.

Student B: Read the information on page 144.

You should then exchange information with your partner to have a complete picture of Saudi Arabia and the recommendations and obligations for visitors to that country. Make notes of the main points of information your partner gives you.

> The largest group of visitors to Saudi Arabia are the thousands of Muslims who visit the holy cities of Mecca and Medina annually. It is important to remember that no non-Muslim is allowed in either of these cities. The country is largely a desert situated on a central plateau. It is best to visit outside the summer because of the extreme heat: in July temperatures can reach 47°C in the interior.
>
> The language is Arabic and visitors should learn the traditional Arab greeting 'Salaam' ('As salaam alaykum') which means 'Peace be upon you'. Another Arabic word to learn is 'insh'allah' ('God willing'). The capital city is Riyadh but any tourist should also try to visit the port of Jeddah and see the Rub al Khali, the Empty Quarter desert.

Student A: Find out from your partner about:
population, cost of living, religion, eating.

UNIT 14 Stage two page 129

Activity

Advice for Travellers

1 Discussion

Work in pairs.

How long do you think it takes to make these journeys by air?

| London | to | New York | Paris | to | Rio de Janeiro |
| Tokyo | to | San Francisco | Madrid | to | Athens |

Look at the photograph and make a list of the disadvantages of travelling long distances by plane. Try to make recommendations for how to deal with these.

2 Listening

Listen to the talk about air travel. Which of the disadvantages and recommendations on your list are mentioned?

Listen to the talk again and note down the advice the speaker gives to air travellers. Use these headings to help you:

Food • Sleep • Seats • Clothes • Shoes • Drinking

3 Mini project

Give a short talk to the class about another country you have visited, or a place in your own country which is not your home town. Collect as much information as you can: photographs, maps, typical products etc. Use these to illustrate your talk. Make sure you make recommendations to the other students in case they go to the place you are talking about. The other students should take notes and ask questions when the talk has finished.

4 Writing

With the information you prepared for your talk, write an article about the place you selected, with recommendations for potential visitors.

Language review

1 The Second Conditional

● **Form**

if + Past Simple followed by *would/could/might* + infinitive.

EXAMPLE: *If I had enough money, I'd buy a computer.*

The example above refers to an unreal situation, as I *don't* have enough money and I *can't* buy a computer. The Second Conditional is often used with an imaginary situation to talk about what we would like: wishes, desires, dreams. It refers to the present and the future. Even though we use the Past Simple, the meaning is *not* past.

Remember that we can reverse the order of conditional sentences without changing the meaning. If we start with the *'would* clause', there is no comma between the two parts of the sentence:

I'd buy a computer if I had enough money.

Would, could and *might* with the Second Conditional express different degrees of possibility:

If I had the chance, I would work abroad. (I would definitely do it in this situation)

If I earned more, I could afford to buy a car. (I could buy the car if I wanted to do it)

If I met the right kind of person, I might get married. (This would be a possibility but I might stay single)

(Compare Language review 2, page 113 - The First Conditional)

2 Recommendations and obligations

● **Recommendations** (general rather than personal advice)

We use *should/shouldn't* and *ought/oughtn't* to for general advice:

You should enjoy a long soak.
You ought not to miss the chance of visiting Kyoto.

Both of these are simply recommendations which do not have to be followed.

If we want the recommendation to be stronger, we can use words like *never, not ever* and *always*:

You shouldn't ever interrupt a Japanese businessman during a meeting.
You should always get to the airport an hour before the flight leaves.
You ought never to carry all your money on you on holiday.

Notice that the following expressions can also be used to make recommendations:

It's important to remember that …
It's a good idea to take light, comfortable clothes during the summer.
It's worth trying to learn a few Japanese phrases.
It's better to stay in a traditional inn or 'Ryokan'.
It's advisable to take traveller's cheques instead of cash.

● **Obligations**

We use *have to* and *must* to express obligations:

Whenever you go into a Japanese house, you must take off your shoes.
In Japan you have to drive on the left-hand side of the road.

Here it is important to do what the person says.

3 Articles

● ***The***

We use *the* when we already know what is being talked about:

In summer the country is extremely hot and humid.

From the text we know *the country* is Japan. In the same way the text talks about sleeping *on **the** floor*, as we know this means the floor in the hotel room. *The* is therefore normally used to refer to a specific thing or person.

We also use *the* when there is only one of something:

From Tokyo you can get to Kyoto in 3 hours on the 'Shinkansen' super-express. (This is the only super-express)

Tokyo is the capital of Japan. (There is only one capital)

We use *the* when we talk about nationalities:

The Japanese are extremely polite and hospitable.
The British are rather reserved.

The text says: *Japan can be confusing for the visitor.*

In this case, where we use *the* + a singular noun, we mean visitors in general not one particular visitor. In the same way we can say:

The dolphin is an extremely intelligent animal. (All dolphins are like this)

● ***A/An***

Remember that we use *a/an* when we mention something for the first time:

We booked a tour with a travel agency but the same tour was 30% cheaper in the hotel.

We say *a tour* the first time, but the second time it is mentioned we say *the tour* because then we know which tour we are referring to.

UNIT 14 Language review   page 131

UNIT 15

Opener

◆ Match these titles with the 'stills' from famous films:

The Invisible Man ☐   Tarzan ☐   Star Wars ☐   E.T. ☐

Snow White ☐   Who Framed Roger Rabbit? ☐

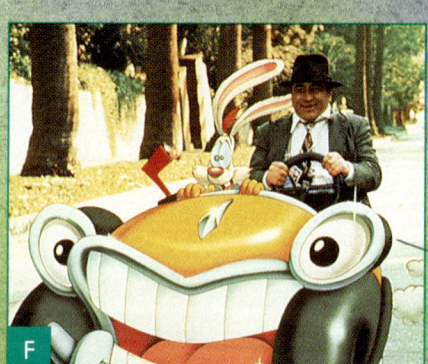

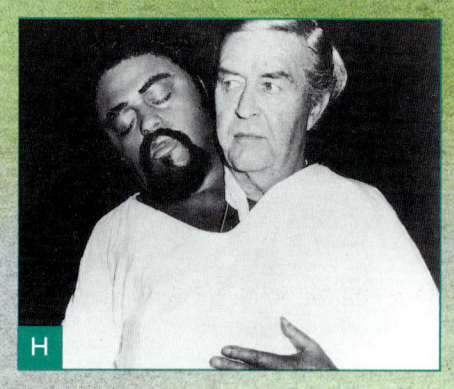

King Kong ☐   The Thing with Two Heads ☐

◆ When do you think each film was made? Guess the dates, and then compare guesses with a partner.

◆ What techniques or special effects are used in these films? How do you think the film-makers created these effects? Discuss one or two of the films with a partner.

page 132 UNIT 15 Opener

Stage one

Moving Images

1 Listening

Listen to these three short conversations. Which of the films in the Opener are the people discussing? Make a note of the three film titles.

Listen again and fill in the gaps in these extracts from the conversations.

1 Apparently, the film was ___shot___ with the real ___people___ and then the cartoons were ___drawn___ later.
2 They ___filmed___ the model ape and the girl separately, and then the two films were ___put___ together.
3 It's just a lifelike ___plastic___ model which is ___stuck___ on to the actor's shoulder.

2 Clues

Listen to the recording again and pick out the clues which helped you to decide which films were being discussed. Make a note of these clues in a table like this. (One clue has been filled in for you.)

Conversation	Film	Clues
1		
2		it was a real ape
3		

3 Vocabulary

Look at the tapescript for Exercise 1 on page 155. Which words or phrases in the conversations are used to mean the following?

1 the fictional people in a film
2 to make a film
3 camera shots which are taken very near to an object or person
4 camera shots which are taken a long way from objects or people
5 characters, objects or scenes which are drawn by an artist
6 a small part of a film shot in one place

● **Words in context**

Guess the meaning of these words from the other words in the same sentence:

1 They really look *three-dimensional*, you know as if the people are talking to them and touching them.
2 They built a *miniature* city, and the model was filmed walking around it.
3 It's just a *lifelike* plastic model which is stuck on to the actor's shoulder.

4 Passive verbs
(Language review 1, page 140)

Compare these two sentences:

A *600 artists produced more than two million drawings for Snow White.*
B *More than two million drawings were produced for Snow White.*

Do both sentences contain the same information? (Do they both give you answers to *what*, *who*, and *how many* questions?)

What do you think is the most important fact in each sentence?

How are the verb forms different?

Read these sentences. Are they like Sentence A or Sentence B?

1 At the end of the film King Kong was killed. ☐
2 Steven Spielberg directed *E.T.* ☐
3 The part of Crocodile Dundee was played by Paul Hogan. ☐
4 *Who Framed Roger Rabbit?* was made in 1988. ☐
5 The cartoon characters in *Roger Rabbit* were drawn after the shooting of the live action. ☐
6 Richard Williams drew the cartoon characters in *Roger Rabbit*. ☐

UNIT 15 Stage one page 133

5 Practice

As you read these extracts from video blurbs, underline or make a list of the B-type (passive) verbs.

EXAMPLE:

Slipstream
Cert. PG

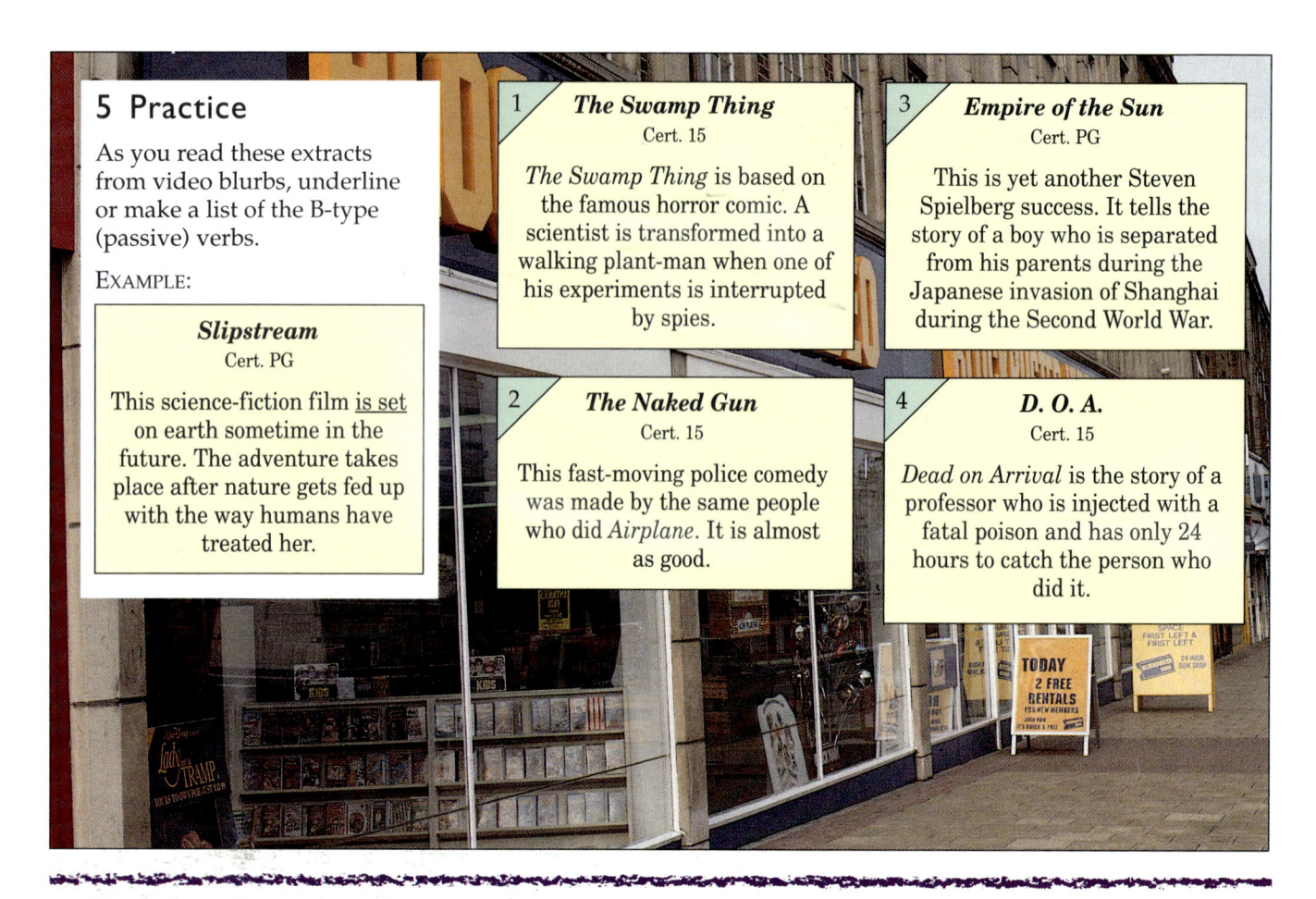

This science-fiction film <u>is set</u> on earth sometime in the future. The adventure takes place after nature gets fed up with the way humans have treated her.

1 The Swamp Thing
Cert. 15

The Swamp Thing is based on the famous horror comic. A scientist is transformed into a walking plant-man when one of his experiments is interrupted by spies.

2 The Naked Gun
Cert. 15

This fast-moving police comedy was made by the same people who did *Airplane*. It is almost as good.

3 Empire of the Sun
Cert. PG

This is yet another Steven Spielberg success. It tells the story of a boy who is separated from his parents during the Japanese invasion of Shanghai during the Second World War.

4 D. O. A.
Cert. 15

Dead on Arrival is the story of a professor who is injected with a fatal poison and has only 24 hours to catch the person who did it.

6 Rewriting

Rewrite the four review extracts using only A-type (active) verbs. In some cases you will have to change several words.

EXAMPLE: **Slipstream**

This science-fiction film takes place on earth ...
or
The makers of Slipstream set this science-fiction film on earth ...

7 The worst film I've ever seen

What is the worst film you have ever seen? What was the story? Write a short summary like this:

From Hell It Came

A young South Sea islander dies and is reincarnated as a tree. The walking tree, with the dead man's face, wanders round the island eating people and destroying villages.

Some of the most famous 'bad films' are:

Teenagers from Outer Space   *The Nasty Rabbit*
Attack of the Killer Tomatoes   *The Green Slime*
Zontar the Thing from Venus   *From Hell It Came*

Have you seen any of them?

In groups of three, find out about the worst films your partners have ever seen. Ask questions about the story.

page 134   UNIT 15 Stage one

8 Writing: review

Write a short review (about 75 words) of a film, a video, or a television programme you have seen recently. You can choose one you enjoyed or one you thought was terrible. Include these details:

1 the subject and a brief outline of the story
2 the best part / the worst part
3 the main reasons you enjoyed it/didn't enjoy it

Use some of the texts in this unit as examples of review styles.

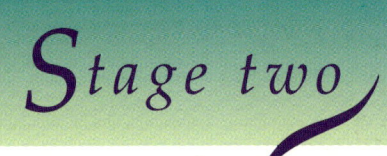

Stage two

What a Waste!

1 Reading

What happens to household rubbish in your country? Is any of it recycled?

Read the text below, which describes some of the most common ways of getting rid of rubbish. Which of these ways do you think is the least harmful to the environment? Discuss your ideas with a partner.

Incineration on land
Household waste can be incinerated. Although this process produces energy, it also causes air pollution, particularly when a lot of plastic is contained in the waste.

Roadside dumping
Old furniture, fridges, televisions and even cars are left at the roadsides by people who can't be bothered to get rid of them properly.

Garden bonfires
Bonfires in back gardens are probably the most dangerous way of getting rid of domestic waste. Poisonous gas is produced when plastics are burnt.

Incineration at sea
So as not to pollute the land, chemical waste is often burnt at sea in incinerator ships. But both the atmosphere and the sea are being polluted.

Dumping at sea
The sea is being used more and more as a dumping place for sewage and nuclear and industrial waste. This method is cheap and easy, but the waste can poison fish, and nuclear waste will remain radioactive for thousands of years.

Landfill sites
Because it is expensive to transport, most household rubbish is buried under the ground. This waste in landfill sites soon pollutes soil and water supplies.

UNIT 15 Stage two   page 135

● **Understanding**

Read the texts again and find the attractions and the dangers of each method of waste disposal. You may have to guess some answers. Fill in a table like this:

Method	Attractions	Dangers
1 Incineration on land		
2 Roadside dumping	easy	public safety/ visual pollution
3 Garden bonfires		
4 Incineration at sea		
5 Dumping at sea		
6 Landfill sites		

2 Vocabulary

Find pairs of words in the list below which both mean:

burn • domestic • dump
get rid of • household
incinerate • rubbish • waste

1 things or stuff we throw away _____ _____
2 to destroy something by fire _____ _____
3 to throw away _____ _____
4 from or belonging to people's homes _____ _____

3 Passive verbs
(Language review 1, page 140)

In Stage 1 (Exercise 4), A-type sentences had active verbs and B-type sentences had passive verbs.

Make a list of the passive verbs used in the texts in Exercise 1. Write them under these headings:

Simple tenses	Continuous tenses	Modals
is dumped	is being dumped	can be dumped

Now compare these two sentences:

Three million tonnes of acid are thrown away by industry each year.
Most household rubbish is buried under the ground.

In the first sentence the writer mentions who throws away the acid: industry.

In the second sentence, why do you think we are not told who buries household rubbish? Try rewriting this as an active sentence.

Compare ideas with a partner.

4 Back to the future
(Language review 1, page 140)

Read this extract from the introduction to a book about the environment.

What does the author think is the most dangerous change that is taking place?

> Our planet is in great danger. All over the world deserts are advancing. Forests are being destroyed at an alarming rate. Lakes, rivers and even seas are being poisoned and polluted. Perhaps most seriously of all, the air that we have to breathe is being changed dramatically, for the worse.

Imagine that everyone starts taking environmental pollution seriously and that, by the year 2020, all the damage has stopped. Rewrite the text as past history, using past tense verbs. Start like this:

In the early 1990s, our planet was in great danger. All over the world deserts were advancing …

The writer does not say who or what is causing the damage to the earth. Rewrite the text using only active verbs. Make it clear who, in your opinion, is responsible for the damage.

5 Listening

Listen to these five people saying what they think should be done to improve the environment. What aspects of the environment are they talking about?

Do you agree or disagree (√ or x) with the five speakers?

	Aspect	Agree/Disagree
A		
B		
C		
D		
E		

6 Predictions

Listen to the five speakers again. What do you think they were going to say next?

A People should travel …

B I think more money should be spent on alternative forms of energy, like …

C I think people …

D It certainly shouldn't be buried or …

E Industries and individuals should be fined for …

Compare your predictions with a partner.

Now listen to a complete version of what the five speakers said. Check your predictions.

Listen again and make a list of the opinion phrases used by the speakers.

EXAMPLE: *I think …*

7 Your opinions
(Language review 2, page 140)

Work in pairs. Make five suggestions of your own for ways in which the environment could or should be protected. Make sentences like this:

I think all private cars should be banned. (Very strong opinion)
or
Public transport could be improved. (An idea or suggestion)

Put these five suggestions in order of importance.

Discuss your ideas with another pair of students.

8 Pronunciation

A compound noun is a noun made from two other words.

Find the compound nouns in the following sentences.

1 I think it's terrible that people dump their rubbish at the roadsides.
2 This waste in landfill sites soon pollutes water supplies and soil.
3 The average household throws away two bins of rubbish a week.
4 Thirty per cent is paper and cardboard.
5 Pollution is a danger to all forms of wildlife as well as to human beings and plants.

Now listen to the same five sentences. Underline the part of the compound nouns that is stressed.

Here are definitions of some more compound nouns. What are they?

6 The person who delivers letters to people's houses
7 The most popular sport in the world
8 You read this to find out what is happening in the world
9 Your father's mother
10 A writing machine

Make sentences using these words. Read them to your partner.

Check that your partner stresses the correct part of the compound nouns he or she reads to you.

UNIT 15 Stage two   page 137

Activity

Let's Get Rid of It

1 Introduction

Make a list of all the substances and things that make up your household rubbish. Use the illustration for ideas and list everything under these headings:

Glass	Paper	Metal	Organic matter	Plastic	Other

2 Discussion
Work in pairs.

- Compare lists with your partner.
- Decide which of these different kinds of rubbish could be used again (recycled).
- Discuss ideas about what should be done with things that cannot be recycled.

3 Role play
Work in groups of four.

There has been a lot of discussion recently in your town about the problem of household and industrial waste. A public meeting is being held to try and reach an agreement on what should be done.

Students A and B: Turn to page 144.

Students C and D: Read these instructions.

Student C
Your family owns a garage in the town and employs 20 mechanics. The garage sells petrol and new cars, but most of the work is on car repairs.

Student D
As a local politican, you are on a committee which plans public spending. The local council currently spends 10% of its budget on waste collection and disposal.

- Write a few notes to refer to during the meeting.
- Discuss the town's problem of waste disposal in groups of four. Try to reach an agreement about what action should be taken.

4 Writing

Write a letter to your local newspaper expressing your *own* opinions about the problem you have just discussed. Make sure you describe the problem, say how serious you think it is and suggest what should be done.

Read what your partners have written. Do you agree? Could you add your signature to their letters?

UNIT 15 Activity   page 139

Language review

1 Passive verbs

● The difference between active and passive sentences

The subject of an active verb is the person (or thing) who does the action:

Mark Chapman killed John Lennon.

Mark Chapman is the subject of the active verb *killed*. John Lennon is the object of the verb.

The subject of a passive verb is the person (or thing) who is affected by the action:

John Lennon was killed by Mark Chapman.

John Lennon is the subject of the passive verb *was killed*. Mark Chapman is the agent of the verb.

● Passive verb forms

Form passive verbs like this:

the verb *to be* + the past participle (the part of the verb used for the Present Perfect).

EXAMPLES: Active infinitive   Passive infinitive

    to kill   to be killed
    to make   to be made
    to know   to be known

There are passive forms of most verb tenses. Here are some examples:

Present Simple: *Fiat cars are made in Italy.*
Past Simple: *Hamlet was written by Shakespeare.*
Present Continuous: *We are being followed.*
Past Continuous: *The car was being driven too fast.*
Future with *will*: *Next year I'll probably be given a new job.*

Use passive infinitives after modal verbs:

Some birds can be taught to talk.
Murderers should be sent to prison.
Environmental pollution mustn't be allowed to continue.

● Use of passive verbs

Use passive verbs when:

1 … the action and the person affected by the action are more important than the agent:

Have you heard the news? John Lennon has been murdered.

2 … you don't know or can't reveal the identity of the agent:

John Lennon was shot yesterday by an unknown assassin.

3 … the agent is unimportant:

Ex-Beatle John Lennon was murdered in New York in December 1980.

2 Expressing personal opinions

Remember these ways of expressing opinions:

I think (that) …
In my opinion …
If you ask me, …
As I see it, …

Use *should* for strong opinions which express advice or recommendations:

If you ask me, people who drink and drive should go to prison.
In my opinion everyone should learn to speak at least one foreign language.

Use *could* for less strongly held opinions which express suggestions:

I think you could work a bit harder.
If you ask me, the government could do more to control pollution.

COMMUNICATION ACTIVITIES

Character Analysis (Unit 1, page 11)

Read about the doodle most like your partner's.

Type 1

You have a keen analytical mind. You are an intelligent thinker. You are a good planner and organiser. Unfortunately you are not easy to work with - you often criticise people who are not as clever as you. There is not much humour or warmth in your doodle.

Type 3

Your doodles show you are a sociable person. You like living and working with other people. You have a very busy private life and you don't worry too much about your work. The faces in your doodle show that you like being the centre of attention.

Type 5

You have a very active personality. You prefer doing things to talking. You try not to have arguments with other people. You are an independent kind of person and you love adventures. You are happiest when you are on your own or with a few good friends.

Type 2

These stars, flowers and circles show you have a lively, interesting mind. You can communicate well and have lots of good ideas. You are sensitive and responsible.

Type 4

You are a nervous person and you sometimes feel like a prisoner. You are a hard worker, but you worry too much, and often have negative thoughts. It is not easy for you to show your feelings.

Is there any truth in this description of your partner's personality? Discuss your ideas.

Mitchells Under Threat (Unit 2, page 21)

Student A: Read these instructions:

You always used to do your shopping at Mitchells, but now you find it much more convenient to shop at an out-of-town supermarket, where there is a wider choice of things to buy. You approve of the plan to build new offices in Kingsworth.

Write a letter to the editor of *The Globe*. Explain why you think the office block should be built. Start like this:

When you have written your letter, turn back to page 21.

```
The Editor,                          Your address
The Globe,
High Street,
Kingsworth

                                     Date

Dear Sir/Madam,

   I was interested to read your lead story
about the plan to replace Mitchells with an
office block. I always used to shop ...

Yours faithfully,

          (Signature)

Name in capitals
```

COMMUNICATION ACTIVITIES

Road Accident (Unit 5, page 48)

Conditions:
This was a narrow road with a blind bend. There were road signs telling motorists to drive slowly. In the middle of the road, there were bright white road markins and cats eyes, but it was a dark night and there was no street lighting. The weather was fine, visibility was clear and the road surface was dry.

Sequence of events:
The driver of Car A (The Montego) was a learner driver. On the night of the accident, this learner did not have a qualified driver him. The Montego was travelling at an excessive speed around a blind left-hand bend. It swung onto the opposite side of the road, and collided with the approaching Sierra (Car B), which was on its own side and going at a safe speed.

Burgers or Not? (Unit 6, page 57)

Discussion and writing

Students A and B

Together with many of the residents in your town, you are very excited about the new restaurant plan. You have different reasons for this:

Student A

You like burgers and chips and other kinds of fast food. You think they are good value for money.

Student B

You think the new restaurant will be a good place for young people to meet.

Discuss your opinions with your partner. Try to agree on the arguments in favour of the opening of the new restaurant. You want to persuade other people in the town that you are right.

Write publicity material expressing your points of view. First, decide what kind of publicity to write. Here are some ideas:

– a leaflet to give to people in the street.

– a poster.

– the script for a half-minute TV video (including ideas for pictures).

Now turn back to page 57.

Are You an Optimist or a Pessimist? (Unit 8, page 76)

Questionnaire scores:

1	A:1	B:0	C:2
2	A:0	B:1	C:2
3	A:2	B:1	C:0
4	A:2	B:0	C:1

If you scored 6-8, you are a born optimist. There's nothing wrong with this, but you're probably disappointed rather frequently.

If you scored 4 or 5, you are a realistic, down-to-earth sort of person. You always hope for the best, but are never disappointed if things go wrong.

If you scored 0-3, you are a real pessimist. Try to look on the bright side a bit more often. You'll get more fun out of life.

COMMUNICATION ACTIVITIES

Criminals Overheard
(Unit 11, page 102)

Student A

You recently overheard a conversation between two criminals in a pub. They didn't notice you, but you had a good look at them.

Later you wrote down some notes of the conversation and a short description of each of the men. Student A is a detective and will ask you to describe the men and what they said.

Use the notes opposite to give the descriptions and report the conversation.

Now look at the pictures of suspects on page 102 with your partner. Try to identify the criminals.

> First man – about 35, balding, well-built, dark moustache, wearing black leather jacket, jeans, trainers. Name Jack or Jake.
>
> Second man – older, possibly mid-forties. Short dark hair, sideburns, clean-shaven, glasses. Thin, pale. Blueish sports jacket and khaki trousers. Had a bad cough.
>
> Conversation – talked about robbing house, owner Mr Sainsford the millionaire industrialist. House in N. London – Hampstead. Two revolvers. Going to steal a car. Possibly breaking in 23rd or 24th March, start about 3 a.m. Have complete plan of house and burglar alarms. Know where safe is located. Know family is away then.

Role Play (Unit 13, page 117)

Student A

What are your secret ambitions?

Write a list of some of the interesting things you have always wanted to do, but have never had the time or money for.

EXAMPLES:

> One day I'm going to climb a mountain.
>
> I'd love to parachute from a plane.
>
> I'd really like to sail round the world in a small boat.

When you have written a list of five ambitions, tell your partner about them. You are an optimist. Try to persuade your partner that everything will be alright.

Mini-saga: A Life of Luxury (Unit 13, page 120)

The saga ends: '… mice and rats.'

COMMUNICATION ACTIVITIES

Saudi Arabia (Unit 14, page 129)

Student B

Saudi Arabia has a population of about 9 million people. It has one quarter of the world's reserves of oil and this has brought vast wealth to the country. For this reason, Riyadh is one of the most expensive cities in the world, so any visitor should be prepared for very high prices. As Saudi Arabia is a strict Muslim country, alcohol is forbidden, so any visitor ought to be aware of this. During the month of Ramadan, Muslims fast during the hours of daylight. In a traditional Arab meal you should eat with your right hand. Any tourist should try camel milk, 'kapsa' (lamb in dark brown rice), dates and of course Arab coffee. Pork is not allowed by Islamic law.

Now turn back to page 129 and find out from your partner about: geography, capital and main cities, climate, useful phrases in Arabic, places to visit.

Let's Get Rid of It (Unit 15, page 138)

Student A

Your family lives on a housing estate near to the industrial part of the town. Many of your neighbours work in local factories and a lot of children live on the estate.

Write a few notes to refer to during the meeting. Now turn back to page 138.

Student B

You are a student at the local college. You have read a lot about environmental pollution, and you are thinking of joining an organisation like Greenpeace.

TAPESCRIPTS

Unit 1, Stage one, 1

1 I'm 21 and I come from Spain. I work in a hotel as a receptionist. I've got dark curly hair and brown eyes. My face is round. What else can I say about myself? I have to look my best for work, so I usually wear make-up - but not too much.

2 I come from Algeria and I'm nearly 23. I'm still a student. Er ... I don't know how to describe myself. I'm quite tall, I've got short dark hair - I'm starting to go bald - oh yes, and I've got a moustache.

3 I'm quite tall for a girl. My hair's long and dark and I usually wear it tied back to keep it out of my eyes. I've got a rather square face. I don't often wear make-up because I prefer to look natural, but I always wear earrings. Oh yes, I'm French and I'm 25.

4 At the moment I'm still 20 years old, but my birthday is next week. I suppose I'm rather short for a man - no-one in my family is tall. I've got short dark hair and brown eyes. I'm short-sighted, so I sometimes wear glasses. I live in Bolivia and I'm a medical student.

5 I'm from Bilbao in the Basque region of Spain. I'm just 22 years old. I'm a primary school teacher. How shall I describe myself? Well, I'm very short. I've got wavy fair hair. My skin is pale and my eyes are greyish - that's rather unusual for someone from Bilbao. I speak two languages - Basque and Spanish.

Unit 1, Stage one, 7

A What does Maria do at the weekends? I never see her around.

B On Saturday she catches the bus into town and looks round the shops. She sometimes meets David and they have lunch together. On Saturday evening she nearly always stays in and studies. She's very hard-working, you know. On Sunday she goes to church, and then makes lunch for everyone. In the evening she reads a book or watches television. She gets on very well with the family.

Unit 1, Stage two, 1

Presenter: Ladies and gentlemen, my first guest this evening is the biologist David Connolly. David is perhaps best known for his interest in environmental issues, but he also teaches at Cambridge University, writes books and newspaper articles, and appears regularly on radio and television. Tell me David, what are you doing these days?

David: Well Mike, I'm making a new television series about wildlife in Britain. You know, we're losing rare animals, birds and plants at an incredible rate. We must do something about it. We have to say quite simply 'Enough is enough.'

Presenter: My next guest is a singer who needs no introduction. She's currently appearing in the American hit musical Starshine. Ladies and gentlemen, please give a warm welcome to Danielle Davidson.

Danielle, tell me, are you happy to be back in London?

Danielle: Generally speaking, yes. I'm enjoying the show because I love British audiences, and I love all your parks and open spaces. But the traffic in London is almost as bad as in New York.

Presenter: Starshine is a wonderful show, Danielle, but you must be exhausted. I mean, every evening you're on stage for nearly two hours without a break.

Danielle: I must admit, I'm getting a little tired, Mike. But it's my job. It's not too bad, you know. I get up late and I take it easy during the day.

Unit 2, Stage one, 1

1 We used to go to relatives in South Wales, and going there on the steam train was really exciting. In those days it was an eight-hour journey from London. My father was always late. I remember staggering along the platform loaded with luggage just as the train was leaving. These days Cyprus is a great favourite, though it's getting a bit too crowded. I adore France, and last year we spent time exploring Provence. I love driving through the country, and a small camper van is ideal for the kids.

2 When I was a child, we lived on the south coast of England. Holidays were usually - though not every year - visits to the family in Ireland, where for two or three weeks I just messed around very pleasantly. At that time nobody went abroad for holidays. These days I go all over the world. The year before last I went to Portugal to play golf.

3 We all used to pile into my Dad's old Ford and go to Brighton for two weeks. We stayed in a hotel which wasn't five-star but was posh enough. Then my mother heard that one of our neighbours had been on holiday to a place called Boulogne. Now we regularly go to Spain - between Marbella and Gibraltar. The food's wonderful and we have a lot of good friends there. We always have fantastic holidays.

Unit 2, Stage one, 6

Conversation 1

A Did you do anything interesting yesterday?
B Yes, I watched the Lendle-Becker match on television. It started at 2 o'clock and went on for nearly three hours.
A Who won?
B Becker. He played really well.

Conversation 2
Sue: Hi, Annie, it's Sue.
Annie: Sue, how nice to hear from you! Did you have a good weekend?
Sue: Lovely. We visited some old friends. Do you remember Jeff and Mary? They moved to North Wales last year. We stayed with them in their new cottage.
Annie: It sounds very relaxing. We had a terrible weekend. I wanted to play tennis on Saturday, but it rained all day. Then we decided to go to the theatre in London, but we missed the train.
Sue: How awful!
Annie: Sunday wasn't much better. We just did lots of jobs around the house. Dave cleaned the car and then finished writing an article for the local newspaper, and I started decorating the living-room.

Unit 2, Stage two, 5

1   A   Remember when it was the Rose and Crown?
    B   It was always full of noisy men who ate too much.
    C   And you waited 10 minutes before you bought your drink.
    D   Never anywhere to sit.

2   D   Then it changed into Kath's Café.
    B   It was still full of noisy men - mostly lorry drivers.
    A   Or workers from the building site.
    C   They only bought greasy food like fish and chips.

3   A   Then Mrs Bradshaw found it and made it into Betty's Tea Shop.
    C   Tea and cakes cost a fortune.
    D   It was always empty.
    C   That was because nobody could afford the prices.

4   B   And then a French couple took it over and called it Chez Nous.
    C   My brother went there once. Apparently, the couple weren't really French at all.
    B   They never closed till after midnight.
    C   When the last customers arrived they always heard a dreadful row.

5   A   Now it's the Burger Palace.
    B   It never closes, and everybody leaves their litter in the street.
    C   D'you remember when it was a little old pub?
    D   Oh yes - The Rose and Crown - those were the days!

Unit 3, Stage one, 3

lovely   beautiful   surrounded   intense   cathedral

interest   motorway   countryside   polluted   located   cultural   industry   excellent   attractive   industrial   crowded   lively   outskirts   minutes   restaurant

Unit 3, Stage one, 11

John: 779 2904
Mark: Hello John. It's Mark.
John: Ah good. You're still coming for supper, aren't you?
Mark: Oh yes. We've already got some wine.
John: Great. Let me tell you how to get here. You coming by bus?
Mark: No, Barbara's got her car.
John: O.K. It'll only take about 15 minutes. It's very easy really.
Mark: Er, we know our way to the centre.
John: Right. From there you go over the bridge and there's a roundabout.
Mark: Ah yes.
John: You take the second exit off the roundabout, into London Road. O.K.?
Mark: London Road.
John: Go straight on for, um, about a mile.
Mark: Straight for one mile.
John: You go past a cinema on your left and then you come to some traffic lights.
Mark: Cinema ... traffic lights. Right.
John: After the traffic lights, take the second road on the right and then the first turning on your left.
Mark: Second right and first left.
John: That's Green Street and the house is half way down on the left.
Mark: That should be O.K. We'll see you about 8.30.

Unit 3, Stage two, 1

1   Well I've had this one for about 10 years now. It's made of wood which is a bit old-fashioned as new ones are made of graphite, I think. It's got a long thin handle with a round head and, um, nylon strings. It's rather heavy but great for my service game.

2   This one's made of plastic. It works with a battery, and it's got a round face and translucent hands and figures you can see in the dark. It makes a horrible loud buzzing sound which it's impossible to ignore. Um, it's the perfect size for taking away when I'm travelling.

3   These are really comfortable and warm. Great for relaxing at the end of the day. I put them on immediately I get home. They're made of wool with rubber soles and they make a funny noise when I walk round the house in them.

4   Um, it's made of glass with a plastic base. It's square-shaped with buttons to adjust the speed. I use it for making soups, milk shakes, and sauces. It saves so much time and it's really easy to use.

Unit 3, Stage two, 4

street   need   thin   tea   hill
grin   easy   me   milk   bit

Dialogue
Jenny: Hello. 21544
Bob: Hi Jenny, it's Bob.
Jenny: Bob! How are you? I haven't seen you for ages.
Bob: No. I've been at a conference in Italy for two weeks.
Jenny: Really? That sounds great. Where were you?

Bob: Milan. Lovely city. Look Jenny, are you free tomorrow evening?
Jenny: Er, it's a bit difficult. I've got to visit my mother.
Bob: Oh well, what about later on? We could go to the cinema maybe.
Jenny: All right, but give me a ring at work just to confirm it, O.K.?
Bob: Yes, I'll phone you around eleven.

Unit 4, Stage one, 1

Joe: Graham. Over here. Pull up a chair.
Graham: Oh hi. Sorry I'm late. Can I get anybody a drink?
Kathy: I think we're all right, thanks. We got you a beer.
Graham: Great. Cheers!
Joe: O.K. What are we going to do? It's a lovely day. Much too nice to be indoors.
Clare: Why don't we have a game of tennis? There are some courts fairly near here.
Kathy: Good idea, Clare. I've got rackets and balls.
Graham: Oh, I'm afraid I'm useless at tennis. I'd prefer to go swimming.
Clare: But it'll be packed with people.
Kathy: Oh, you're right. It's always the same at weekends anywhere you go. I'd rather do something else.
Joe: How about hiring a boat on the river? We could have a picnic lunch.
Graham: That sounds great. We can get some wine and cheese.
Clare: I think we should get some fruit as well.
Graham: Right. We can go swimming too.
Kathy: Well let's go before all the boats disappear. It's nearly 1.15.
Joe: Hey, I can't swim!
Clare: Oh don't worry! We'll look after you.

Unit 4, Stage one, 4

1 It's a lovely clear day.
2 They shouldn't park their car in front of the exit.
3 The station is fairly close to the centre.
4 Are we near a bank?
5 This chair's very uncomfortable.
6 Would you like a beer?
7 Don't disappear. Lunch is almost ready.
8 I haven't been there for ages.
9 How long have you been staying here?
10 She's got lovely hair.

Unit 4, Stage two, 4

1 I'm going to wear a suit to the wedding.
2 I can't think where I left my bag.

Part 2
1 John's been out for ages.
2 If you're going out, can you get me some self-raising flour?

3 What a week! I really need some peace and quiet this weekend.
4 Have a pear. They're really juicy.
5 Look what I bought in the sale. I saved £15!
6 Would you like me to pour you some more coffee?

Unit 4, Activity

Now for local weather in the Lake District. Starting off fine with some sunshine but by early afternoon heavy rain spreading from the west coast will mean it's going to be pretty miserable for outdoor enthusiasts. The bad weather is expected to last for the next 36 hours. Over to you, Liz.

Thank you, Gordon. We've just heard that, due to the forecast of rain, the Cartmel Races have been cancelled. The Cockermouth Agricultural Show is also expected to be badly affected by the weather. The police have asked tourists to be particularly careful about going out sailing this afternoon. If you do go out, well, take an umbrella and a raincoat with you.

Unit 5, Stage one, 6

Interviewer: Andrew, you're quite a hero, aren't you?
Andrew: Am I? I don't know.
Interviewer: Have you ever been on the radio before?
Andrew: No, not really. I mean, I've never found a bomb before.
Interviewer: Tell me what happened that morning.
Andrew: Well, I collected my newspapers at about 8 o'clock, and started my paper round. I went past the phone box and I saw this sort of black bag in one corner. I got off my bike to have a better look. It was just an ordinary briefcase, so I decided to find out who it belonged to.
Interviewer: When did you realise it was a bomb?
Andrew: As soon as I opened it and saw the battery and the wires.
Interviewer: Have you ever seen a bomb before?
Andrew: I've seen them on the telly, that's all.
Interviewer: What did you do next?
Andrew: I rushed out of the box, went to the nearest house and phoned the police.
Interviewer: When did the police arrive?
Andrew: I didn't stay to find out. I had to go and finish delivering my newspapers.
Interviewer: Were you late for school?
Andrew: Only about five minutes. Nobody seemed to mind.

Unit 5, Stage one, 7

1 Have you ever been on the radio before?
2 When did you realise it was a bomb?
3 Have you ever seen a bomb before?
4 What did you do next?
5 When did the police arrive?
6 Were you late for school?

Unit 5, Stage two, 2

Woman
I remember waking up. The roof was falling in around me. While I was searching around for something to put over my head to protect myself, a wooden beam fell on me. My legs were trapped and I couldn't move. I called out for my husband. Luckily he was all right. Then I heard our cat, Claude, miaowing.

Man
I went to bed just after midnight. I was only half-asleep when the wind started blowing. Half an hour later our bedroom window shattered with a terrible crash. I leapt out of bed and rushed to check that the kids were all right. I went into the boys' room and saw Tom - he's my youngest son - staring out of the window. Matthew was still sleeping peacefully. When I went into the girls' bedroom, I could only see Laura - she was calmly getting dressed. Then I heard someone crying. It was Becky - she was hiding under the bed, shaking with fear.

Unit 5, Stage two, 4

1 It was still dark, so I knew it wasn't morning. I could tell something was wrong. The trouble is I was only half awake so I had no idea what was going on. I suppose I just decided the best thing to do was put my clothes on and go downstairs.

2 I heard my brother get out of bed, and I saw him open the curtains. All you could see was big trees swaying in the wind. I think I just turned over and went back to sleep. The next thing I knew, Dad was shaking me and telling me to get dressed.

3 It was absolutely terrifying. First I heard this crash, then I heard Dad shout, and Mum scream. For a few minutes I just lay there wondering what to do. In the end I leapt out of bed and ran to the window. I was standing there watching the storm when Dad burst in.

4 The noise was awful. I thought it was a war or something, so I hid under Laura's bed. I was really scared - I couldn't stop crying and shaking.

Unit 5, Activity

In the early hours of this morning, five people were injured in a car accident just outside the village of Heathfield in East Sussex. The driver of one of the cars, a Montego, and his two passengers were seriously injured in the collision. The driver of the other car, a Sierra, suffered a broken leg, but his passenger, a student from Brighton University, escaped with minor cuts and bruises. East Sussex police are asking anybody who was driving in the Heathfield area between 11.30 and midnight last night to get in touch with them urgently on Heathfield 873257.

Unit 6, Stage one, 1

Conversation 1
A I think it's very worrying. A few years ago they had a campaign against butter - do you remember? They said it was bad for your heart. Now some doctors are saying that the chemicals and colourings in margarine are more dangerous than the fat in butter.
B The trouble is the experts don't even agree with each other. It seems to me that it's impossible for us to …

Conversation 2
A Have you heard the latest report about smoking?
B Do you mean the one about passive smokers?
A Yes, apparently if you live or work with smokers you can get cancer and heart disease.
B In my opinion, they're making a lot of a fuss about nothing. Nobody really knows what causes cancer.
A You're only saying that because you smoke.
B That's not the only reason. And anyway I don't smoke when …

Conversation 3
A Do you want to come jogging at the weekend?
B What me? You're joking!
A Why not? Jogging's good for you.
B I think it's a complete waste of time.
A What do you normally do for exercise?
B Well, I sometimes play …

Conversation 4
A If you ask me, they don't know what they're talking about.
B But everybody knows that sunbathing's bad for you. They've proved it.
A How can they? I just don't understand.
B Don't ask me, I'm not an expert. But they say if you get too much sun …

Unit 6, Stage one, 5

1 A few years ago they had a campaign against butter.
2 They said it was bad for your heart.
3 Have you heard the latest report about smoking?
4 If you live or work with smokers you can get cancer and heart disease.
5 You're only saying that because you smoke.
6 Do you want to come jogging at the weekend?
7 But everybody knows that sunbathing's bad for you.
8 How can they?
9 I'm not an expert.

Unit 6, Stage two, 6

Andrew: Have you heard that Kingburger want to convert the old theatre into a restaurant?
Tom: I think it's quite wrong.
Andrew: So do I. I think it's a beautiful old building.
Tom: I agree.

Cathy: You're making a lot of fuss about nothing. That so-called theatre is actually a cinema now, and it's losing money. I think they should let Kingburger take it over.
Andrew: I don't. Lots of local people want to turn it back into a theatre. Kingburger can use any building. I don't think they should be allowed to use it.
Tom: Neither do I. These burger companies really annoy me. They build ugly restaurants, and then sell people unhealthy food at high prices. I think there are enough burger restaurants already.
Cathy: I'm sorry, I can't accept that. Millions of people all over the world like burgers. McDonald's have even got a restaurant in Moscow. The companies are only giving us what we want.
Tom: Rubbish! I don't think that most people want burgers.
Cathy: I do.

Unit 7, Stage one, 3

1 invitation
2 impractical
3 economics
4 politician

Part 2
a That was a very enjoyable meal.
b Jane positively dislikes people smoking in front of her.
c The noise outside is unbelievable.
d These instructions are far too complicated.
e Have you met Gabriela? She's Argentinian.
f Oh dear. We've got a maths examination next week.
g His mother is a very influential woman.
h I prefer an automatic car. It's much easier to drive.
i Why do you always have to be so uncooperative?
j Sarah wants to be an economist.

Unit 7, Stage two, 1

A Stone Employment Bureau. Graham Brown – can I help you?
B Yes please. I'd like to make an appointment with someone to see about getting a job.
A Fine. I'll just get a few details first.
B O.K.
A Now, could I have your full name please?
B Yes. It's Alison Forde. That's F..O..R..D..E.
A F..O..R..D..E. And your address?
B 27 Wood Road, Lichfield.
A And do you have a phone?
B Well, it's my parents'. 43876.
A Good. Can you come at 11.30 this Thursday?
B Yes, that's fine.
A Oh, and please bring a passport-size photo.

Part 2
Interviewer: What sort of work have you done before, Miss Forde?
Alison: Well, I've worked as a secretary in an engineering company.
Interviewer: But you've been looking for work for about six months now, haven't you?
Alison: Yes, unfortunately the company went bankrupt and closed down last year, so I had to give up my flat in November. Ever since then I've been staying with my parents. (The) trouble is, you can't always depend on your parents, can you?
Interviewer: Well, you're not totally inexperienced. I see you took three 'A' levels at school.
Alison: Yes, history, English and art. Then, when I left school, I did a secretarial course.
Interviewer: You speak French too, don't you?
Alison: Yes. Two years ago I spent six months in France as an au pair. I don't speak it fluently but I can get by. I've been practising a bit at home since I lost my job, but it's very difficult. I've been applying for jobs, but it's useless.
Interviewer: What about hobbies and interests?
Alison: Um, I play a bit of squash. Reading, films. That's about it. I get really bored at home.
Interviewer: Yes. When did you last do any work?
Alison: Oh, six weeks part-time in a supermarket last summer but I didn't like it at all. I really need a permanent job.
Interviewer: Hmm, you may have to look for something in Birmingham or another big town.
Alison: I don't really want to move … but if that's the only way …

Unit 7, Stage two, 3

1 You couldn't give me a hand with this, could you?
2 That was a great film, wasn't it?
3 You're not going to wear that hat, are you?
4 Ah, you took my book, didn't you?
5 He's bought a new car, hasn't he?
6 I think they've gone on holiday, haven't they?
7 She plays the piano really well, doesn't she?
8 We can easily finish this work today, can't we?

Unit 8, Stage one, 2

(Telephone rings)
J.F. Allo.
Belinda: Oh, hello Jean-François, it's Belinda.
J.F. Belinda! How nice to hear from you! I'll be seeing you tomorrow, right?
Belinda: Yes. I've got the contract and I'll get the 8.15 Cross-Channel Express from London.
J.F. O.K. Will you have time for lunch?
Belinda: Definitely. I'll be in Paris at 11. Can you meet me? It's Gare du Nord.
J.F. Sure. I know a very good bistro not far from there. I hope you will be my guest.
Belinda: That sounds lovely. I've got to get the 3.10 to Lyons.
J.F. No problem. I'll give you a lift to the station. It won't be any trouble.
Belinda: Oh, that's very kind of you.
J.F. See you tomorrow then.

(Belinda dials another number)
C.R. Diga.
Belinda: Um, could I speak to Carlos Ramirez, please?
C.R. Speaking. Is that Belinda?
Belinda: Yes. Sorry, I didn't recognise you.
C.R. Don't worry. What time are you getting here tomorrow?
Belinda: I've just spoken to Jean-François. I'm seeing him for lunch and then leaving Paris at 3.10. Then I change trains in Lyons and get the 7.18 to Barcelona.
C.R. 7.18. Hmm, so you'll be here about 10, right?
Belinda: Yes. It seems incredible, doesn't it?
C.R. Oh yes. These new trains are fantastic. O.K., I'll meet you at the station and we'll have some dinner together.
Belinda: Fine. We can talk about the contract then.
C.R. Good. Hasta mañana then.
Belinda: Bye, Carlos.

Unit 8, Stage two, 3

Jenny: We're catching the early morning ferry from Dover to Calais, then as soon as we arrive in France we're going to find a little café and have a real French breakfast. That won't take us very long. We're spending our first night in Paris with some friends. Then on Wednesday we're meeting Mike and Carol just outside Paris, between three and four o'clock in the afternoon.
Diane: Who's driving? You or Dave?
Jenny: Dave's driving most of the time, but I'm going to drive whenever he gets tired.
Diane: Are you camping again?
Jenny: No, not this year. We're renting a cottage. We booked it in January - we weren't going to risk being disappointed like we were two years ago. We're going to cook most of our meals ourselves, though I expect we'll eat in restaurants three or four times while we're there.
Diane: It all sounds fantastic. I hope you enjoy yourselves. Think of me while you're relaxing in your cottage, eating all that fantastic French food.
Jenny: I'll send you a postcard if I remember. Bye!
Diane: Bye! Have a good time.

Unit 8, Stage two, 6

1 You're in the wrong room.
2 Did you hear that bang?
3 Good morning. Can I help you?
4 What are you waiting for?
5 Have you rung your mother yet?

Unit 8, Activity

Good evening. Here is the 6 o'clock news for Tuesday the 5th of July. First the headlines.

60,000 people of Kirishi, a small industrial town near Leningrad, are being slowly poisoned by a chemical factory. Twelve children have already died.

Britain will have to pay between 5 and 8 billion pounds for sea defences over the next 60 years, and could lose its best south-coast beaches.

A leading medical expert has claimed that a quarter of Britain's 15 million smokers will die early unless they join the growing numbers of those giving up.

Unit 9, Stage one, 1

1 **A** Have we got any eggs? They're only £1.20 a dozen this week.
  B I can't remember. I think we've still got three or four left.
  A Okay, let's just get half …

2 **A** Do we really need two jars of coffee?
  B Yes, we do, darling. Yesterday, I had to borrow some Nescafe from the …

3 **A** We haven't got much fruit left, have we?
  B Well, we haven't got many bananas.
  A O.K. How many shall we get?
  B Oh, I don't know. Five or …

4 **A** Have we got enough rice to last until next week?
  B I think so.
  A Don't forget, we're making curry for eight people on Friday.
  B That's a point. We'd better get …

5 **A** Shall we get some apples?
  B How much are they?
  A South African ones are the cheapest. They're 40p a pound.
  B Have they got any English ones?
  A Yes, but they're 55p a pound.
  B Oh, that's okay. I prefer …

6 **A** Look there's a discount on Coke. It's 20p a can, or 90p for a pack of six.
  B We'd better have six – you know how much Coke …

Unit 9, Stage one, 9

1 **Tom:** Is the party this Saturday?
  Ben: No, it's next Saturday.

2 **John:** We need two bags of rice, don't we?
  Paul: No, we need two bags of sugar and one bag of rice.

3 **Jane:** Have we invited eight people to the party?
  Mary: No, we've invited twenty.

4 **Jo:** Did you say you wanted Australian apples?
  Ian: No, I said I wanted French ones.

5 **Mike:** They cost 55p a kilo, don't they?
  Pete: No, they're 55p a pound.

Questions
1 Camembert is from Italy, isn't it?
2 Bratwurst is a kind of German cheese, isn't it?
3 Granny Smiths are pears, aren't they?
4 Tortellini is a kind of bread, isn't it?
5 Cabbage is a kind of fruit, isn't it?
6 Sushi is a Canadian dish, isn't it?

Unit 9, Stage two, 1

1 My saxophone, I suppose. It cost me £600 two years ago, so it's probably worth about 700 now.

2 The only valuable thing I've got is my grandmother's wedding ring. I took it to the jeweller's a few months ago, and they said it was worth between forty and fifty pounds.

3 I haven't got anything very valuable really. There's my stamp collection, but that can't be worth more than about a couple of hundred pounds.

4 My Rolls Royce. I bought it in 1959. I don't know what it's worth now. £25,000 perhaps.

5 That's easy – a photograph of my grandparents when they were very young. It's not worth anything – but it's means a lot to me. It's got great sentimental value.

Unit 9, Activity

Presenter: And, moving right along. Now I think we have Charlie on the line. Hello, Charlie.
Charlie: Hello.
Presenter: How can I help?
Charlie: Well, er, I've got a problem with fruit machines. I can't stop putting money into them. It's costing me more and more money.
Presenter: How much money exactly, Charlie?
Charlie: 'bout £10 a week.
Presenter: Where do you get the money from?
Charlie: Different places. Erm, I use my pocket money, and what I get paid from my Saturday job, and I sometimes borrow from my Mum and Dad.
Presenter: Do you ever win money from the machines?
Charlie: Yes, sometimes, but not very often. The problem is, it's getting worse. I've started skipping school. What do you think I should do?
Presenter: Well, if I were you Charlie …

Unit 10, Stage one, 5

In the years from five to eleven, children develop many physical skills. There can be a great variation in children's height and weight, and there are no hard and fast rules about size or physical ability. In these years, boys and girls are of equal strength and energy and can compete with each other in team games. At around five years, most children can run, climb, jump, ride a tricycle and throw a ball.

By the age of six, they can swing by their arms, skip, and hit and catch large balls.

At seven, most children can coordinate the parts of their body. This means they can balance and change positions in activities like trampolining, gymnastics and bike riding.

Between the ages of eight and ten, children develop the ability to do more complicated activities such as juggling and swimming.

Unit 10, Stage two, 1

Conversation 1
Woman: … you must tell him. He'll see the damage as soon as he gets it out of the garage.
Young man: I suppose so.
Woman: You must offer to pay for a new one.
Young man: How much do headlights cost?

Conversation 2
Man: You mustn't buy them if they aren't wide enough.
Woman: They'll be okay when I've walked round in them for a few days.
Assistant: Sorry to keep you waiting. How are you getting on?
Woman: Fine. I'll have this pair, please. You needn't wrap them up.

Conversation 3
Woman: Look! It isn't yours. You mustn't use it without asking me.
Girl: It was only five minutes.
Woman: That's not the point. I have to pay the bills; you don't.
Girl: Sorry. I'll get him to ring me tomorrow.

Conversation 4
Woman: I think the kitchen is too small.
Man: We don't have to live in the kitchen, do we? What about the rest of it?
Woman: I'd prefer one like Liz and Dave's.
Man: So would I, but theirs is in the middle of town. We can't afford to pay £300 a month, can we?

Unit 10, Stage two, 5

1 You must offer to pay for a new one.
2 We don't have to live in the kitchen …

Part 2
1 I don't want to go to the party.
2 We're catching the bus to the college.
3 She's writing a letter to Michael.
4 I'm taking my coat to the cleaners.
5 I lent him five pounds till tomorrow.

Unit 11, Stage one, 6

1 vegetable   2 baby   3 bright   4 volume
5 verdict   6 ban

Part 2
1 Oh, what a beautiful vase!
2 I don't like a big breakfast.
3 They've never been to Venice.
4 Ben's visiting his brother.
5 That was a marvellous barbecue.
6 Oh dear! I've broken the hoover.

Unit 11, Stage one, 7

A Lawyer: I would like to ask the defendant, did you, on the night of August 26th, break into Smith's Jewellers and steal the antique silver you see here in court?
Defendant: Er … well, yes I did, but I was totally broke you see …

B Reporter: There are still hundreds of people protesting outside Farnham Airforce Base. The police are making an announcement …
Policeman: Attention please! Attention! You have ten minutes to move on. Please leave the area or we will have to take action.

C Reporter: Mr Brown, why wasn't Potter included in the team for this weekend?
Brown: Um, I can't say anything at this stage, I'm afraid. There will be an official announcement later today.

D Announcer: And now we're going over to Jean Smales for the latest traffic news. Hello Jean.
Jean: Hi Gary. Not very good news for drivers in the London area this morning. There's been an accident on the M25 at junction 13 which has caused long queues for northbound traffic. Use alternative routes today if you can.

E Reporter: Sonny, what about a world title fight?
Leonard: Well, I'm ready to fight Clayson any time, any place he wants. I reckon I deserve a chance.

F Reporter: Er, Minister. Is there any truth in the reports of your resignation?
Minister: None whatsoever!

Unit 11, Stage two, 1

1 Hi Paul. Jim Tate here. My car's out of action again. It's with the mechanic, so if I were you I'd go by bus tomorrow.

2 Um, hello Mr Bennet. This is Janet Street phoning from the dentist's. You have an appointment to see Mr Carlisle this Thursday at 5.15.

3 Good evening. This is Eric Davies from Martins Plastics. We're very unhappy about the new contract and we won't sign it unless there are significant changes made.

4 Er, Mr Bennet. It's Mr Haynes from number 17. Your dog has been in my garden again and dug up all my roses. It really is the limit. If you can't keep him under control, I'll have to call the police.

5 Er, Paul, it's me, Phil. I can't make the squash game on Friday. How about Saturday morning at 10.30?

6 Paul. Sarah speaking. Many thanks for inviting us to lunch on Sunday but I'm afraid we won't be able to make it. My mother's coming over the same day. Sorry!

Unit 11, Stage two, 6

Colin: I'm home!
Anne: Colin! In the kitchen!
Colin: Hi darling! I picked up the kids' passports so we're all set for France.
Anne: Oh good. I arranged the medical insurance.
Colin: You didn't! I've already done it.
Anne: But I said I was going to do that.
Colin: No, I told you I was going to do the car insurance and the medical insurance.
Anne: Hang on. You said you'd do the car insurance and book the ferry tickets. You never mentioned anything about medical insurance.
Colin: Yes I did. I definitely told you I'd do it. You said you would collect the traveller's cheques and currency and buy the food. Remember?
Anne: Oh, it doesn't matter. I'll just cancel it. The girl said they were open Saturday mornings. Did you get the suitcase?
Colin: Um, didn't you say you'd do that?

Unit 12, Stage one, 2

Anne: Oh hello Laura. It's Anne. I really need to talk to you.
Laura: What's the problem?
Anne: It's Amy. She's just got engaged.
Laura: Has she? But she's only eighteen!
Anne: Seventeen-and-a-half. I'm not completely old-fashioned but I really think she should hang on. They've only been going out for eight months! What on earth am I going to do?
Laura: Look. You should have a long talk with her. Don't get angry but try and persuade her to wait.
Anne: O.K. That might help. I get on quite well with her really but she's made up her mind. I'll try to have a word with her later.

Part 2

Nick: Hi Anne, it's Nick. Is it true Amy's getting married?
Anne: Oh, don't remind me Nick. I just don't know what to do. She's far too young. Her boyfriend's only nineteen.
Nick: Really! What's he like?
Anne: Oh, nice enough I suppose. His name's Wayne. Smokes like a chimney. Unemployed too. What do you think I should do?
Nick: Hmm. Why don't you talk to both of them? Be helpful and ask them to wait until he's got a job and Amy's finished school.
Anne: I've tried talking to Amy but she just won't listen. She thinks I'm interfering and she says she's in love with him.
Nick: I would try to be patient. They may change their minds if you wait.

Part 3
Anne: Do you mind if I smoke, Ella?
Ella: No, go ahead. Are you still worried about Amy?
Anne: Yes, I am. She's being so stubborn about marrying this guy. Oh, perhaps I shouldn't fight it. It's her life, after all.
Ella: O.K. But you're her mother. Has Paul talked to her?
Anne: Oh yes. But she won't listen. So many young couples are separating or getting divorced these days. She's too young.
Ella: If I were you I'd ring the boyfriend's parents. They probably feel the same way you do.
Anne: Well, it's worth a try. I could have a word with Sharon too. She's Amy's best friend.
Ella: Good idea. Come on! Don't worry. Give Sharon a ring.

Unit 12, Stage one, 6

1 wood 2 walk 3 fork 4 book 5 shook 6 hall

Part 2
1 I thought you weren't coming to the party.
2 Would you like some tea?
3 You shouldn't drive so fast.
4 Paul's a very old friend of mine.
5 There's an interesting talk on the radio tonight.
6 This is a very good restaurant.
7 Let's go for a walk after lunch.
8 James loves cooking.

Unit 12, Stage two, 7

Interviewer: Er, Doctor Edwards, you've talked about several modern health problems but what about stress? Why is it so common nowadays.
Doctor: Well we live in a very stressful world today. If someone has to rush to the office every day, works under a lot of pressure and eats the wrong kind of food, that person will probably suffer from some kind of stress. Of course it depends on their personality. But if the same person doesn't get any exercise, and worries a lot as well, they can easily become stressed. Unless people realise that stress is a factor in our health, they will continue to feel bad and get ill.
Interviewer: I see. But what does stress produce?
Doctor: Oh, there are a large number of different symptoms: headaches, insomnia, poor appetite, a feeling of tiredness and high blood pressure. These are the most common. Oh, and depression as well.
Interviewer: That seems to be an awful lot.
Doctor: Well yes it is. Of course if you're lucky you might never get any of these. On the other hand, sometimes the smallest things can be stress related. I'm thinking of things like indigestion, biting your nails or even feeling bad-tempered.
Interviewer: And is there anything we can do about stress?
Doctor: Oh yes. You can start by improving what you eat and taking more exercise. It also helps to get more sleep. If these are the only things you do, you'll definitely feel a new person.
Interviewer: Is there anything else?
Doctor: Yes. There are three activities which have proved very effective in reducing stress. Firstly, relaxation exercises. These are one of the best things you can do. Secondly, biofeedback, which is simply getting information about your body so you can take action. Finally, there's meditation. If anyone tries these, he or she will certainly feel the benefit.

Unit 12, Stage two, 10

1 Insomnia, poor appetite and a feeling of tiredness are some of the most common symptoms of stress.
2 Sometimes the smallest things can be stress-related.
3 People's biggest concern while they are on holiday is burglary.
4 The best type of holiday for many people is in a hotel.
5 A hotel is usually the most expensive type of accommodation.
6 The weather is often the most important factor for a holiday.

Unit 12, Activity

Caller 1
Oh good evening. My name's David Rogers. I'm 40 years old and married with two small children. I have a good job as an accountant with a big insurance company. My problem is one which I think affects lots of people today. Credit cards. I just can't control myself with them and at the moment I owe hundreds of pounds. Every month I have to pay a huge amount of interest and I can never seem to pay it off. The worst thing is that so many places offer credit. There's no escape. I can hardly afford to pay the family expenses and the credit card at the same time. If I carry on like this I'll never be clear of it. I have three credit cards and, as I'm always short of money, it's very tempting to use them. I've tried to be more careful but it's no good. What should I do?

Caller 2
Hello. This is Millie Anderson. I'd like to tell the panel about my problem. I'm a pensioner and I live alone. Recently some young people moved in next door. Now normally I'm very tolerant and I don't like to complain. Live and let live, I say. But the situation now is intolerable. They have parties all the time with such loud music. One of them plays the electric guitar and practises for hours on end. I don't want any trouble but I'm not sleeping and I don't know what to do. What would the panel advise?

Caller 3
Hi. I'm Teresa Sanderson. Um, I'm 16 and I live with my parents. The problem is that I want to leave school and get a job, have some money and be independent. My parents insist that I stay on at school and go to university, but I'm bored stiff with studying. I'd like to work and live in a flat with a friend. Sometimes I feel like leaving home as

nobody understand the problem. The most frustrating thing is that I'm not very good at school anyway. What would you suggest I do?

Unit 13, Stage one, 1

1 **Simon**: Are you coming on Saturday?
   Jonathan: I might. I haven't made up my mind yet.
   Simon: Come on. It'll be a good game. Last time we played them we scored five goals.
   Jonathan: I'm not sure. I'll give you a ring on Friday.

2 **Jane**: But if we go by car and boat, it'll take us at least two days.
   Anne: You've flown before, haven't you?
   Kate: Yes, but that was ages ago.
   Anne: What exactly are you worried about?
   Kate: I don't know really. Everything, I suppose. We might crash; I might be sick; there might be a storm.
   Jane: There might be a storm if we go by boat. The boat might sink, you might fall overboard, and you'll certainly feel sick.

3 **Helen**: You haven't made any definite plans, then?
   Liz: No, not yet. John loves hot weather, so we may go to North Africa again.
   Helen: You don't sound very keen.
   Liz: I'm not. The trouble is, I prefer sightseeing to lying on crowded beaches.
   Helen: Isn't there somewhere you'd both like? What about Italy?
   Liz: It's funny you should say that. I thought I might go somewhere on my own this year – perhaps Northern Italy.
   Helen: Wouldn't John mind?
   Liz: I suppose he might. Who knows?

4 **Mike**: Do you still feel fed up?
   Dave: Yes, I had a chat with my boss last week as you suggested.
   Mike: And?
   Dave: I'm afraid it didn't do any good.
   Mike: So what are you going to do?
   Dave: Well, I'm definitely going to resign at the end of next week.
   Mike: Then what?
   Dave: I don't know. I'll probably have a holiday, then I may apply for something abroad – possibly in computers, or I may even go back to university.

5 **Julie**: That colour really suits you.
   Maria: Do you think so? It isn't too bright, is it?
   Julie: No, it's fantastic! Don't you like it, then?
   Maria: Yes, I love it, but Tony might think it's too short. Maybe I'll buy this one instead.

Unit 13, Stage one, 5

1 It'll take us at least two days.
2 You'll certainly feel sick.
3 I thought I might go somewhere on my own.
4 I'm definitely going to resign.
5 I may apply for something abroad.

Part 2

I spent all weekend in bed.
I was sure I was going to die.
I've never felt so ill in my life.
On Sunday morning I decided to phone the doctor.
He gave me some pills and told me to stay off work.

Unit 13, Activity

1 I'm really involved in the lives of the characters. To me they're real people – they're like friends.

2 I know it's stupid, but when you've had a long hard day at work, you just want to come home and sit down and watch the telly. You don't have to think when you're watching *Neighbours*.

3 I've watched *Dynasty* ever since it started. It's a habit, I suppose. I always make sure I'm in on Wednesday nights. It gives me something to look forward to in the middle of the week.

4 To start with I thought *Dallas* was silly – I used to watch it for a laugh – then I got interested in the story. Now, I watch it because I hate JR – he's such a horrible character. I just sit there watching him and hating him.

5 I haven't got a favourite - I watch all the soaps. They make you forget your own problems.

Unit 14, Stage one, 2

Gary Taylor
I left school as soon as I could when I was 15. I spent four years working in a factory, and then I was out of work for a bit, and I've been a bus driver for about, er, three and a half years, I think. Yes. Um, bus driving is badly paid, boring and tiring. If I had the time and money, I might do some sort of training course. I'd really like to be a plumber or a gardener. We've lived in a two-bedroomed council flat since we were married. It's not in very good condition, and the neighbourhood is a bit run down but we can't afford to move anywhere else. My wife's got a part-time job but it's never enough to make ends meet. All our money goes on rent, electricity, gas and the kids. If I could afford it, I'd buy Margaret a watch; it's years since I gave her a present.

Eileen Smythe
I've never really had to worry about money. If I had to be careful about how much I spent, I don't know what I would do. I went to private school and college. I took a degree in economics and then I joined the foreign section

page 154 | TAPESCRIPTS

of a merchant bank where I've been ever since. On the whole my job is interesting and challenging. I earn a good salary and share an apartment in New York with a friend. I would love to work abroad if I had the chance to have a change of scene and learn a language. I enjoy being single but I might consider getting married if I met the right kind of guy.

Annie McStay
I'm a Supervisor in a supermarket. I really like working with people and dealing with customers. I've been with the company for 20 years in total. I work a 38-hour week and we have enough to get by on. We've always lived in the same house: a three-bedroomed semi with a garden. We're all very keen on gardening in our family. If we had enough money, I'd love to go on a cruise but that's wishful thinking. Fortunately my children have both done well. My daughter is at university studying languages and my son has a good job in a travel agents. I'm very proud of them both. Of course if I had a bit more money I wouldn't complain but I'll never be a millionaire, that's for sure!

Unit 14, Stage two, 6

1 If you eat all that cake, you'll feel sick.
2 You shouldn't miss the chance to try sushi.
3 If you're driving in Britain, it's necessary to drive on the left.
4 If you're travelling by plane, it's not a good idea to eat too much.
   or
   If you're travelling by plane, it isn't a good idea to eat too much.
5 If he comes early we'll go to the cinema.
6 I'd go to Hawaii if I had enough money.
7 I wouldn't lose my temper if I were you.

Unit 14, Activity

Today more and more people are travelling by plane for holidays and business. Everyone tries to tell us that flying is quick, convenient and even glamorous but it's usually just the opposite. How many times are flights delayed or overbooked? The seats are cramped and uncomfortable, the food is usually awful and it's almost impossible to sleep. Then for long flights there's also the problem of jet-lag. So what can you do to make your journey more pleasant? You should always wear comfortable clothes and shoes. In fact you really ought to take your shoes off to really relax. It's probably better to eat very little and you shouldn't drink alcohol as it's much stronger at high altitudes. Stick to plenty of mineral water or soft drinks, to prevent dehydration. It's a good idea to sleep if you can, and it's worth trying to get a seat with more leg room, for example near the emergency exits.

Unit 15, Stage one, 1

1 A The characters look so real. I mean how did they do it?
  B I watched a programme about it on television. Apparently, the film was shot with the real people and then the cartoons were drawn later.
  A But they really look three-dimensional – you know, as if the people are talking to them and touching them.

2 A At the beginning in the jungle, I think it was a real ape, but for the close-ups, they used a moving model.
  B Are you sure? What about the way it grabs the girl?
  A That was just trick photography. They filmed the model ape and the girl separately, and then the two films were put together.
  B And what about the New York scenes at the end?
  A They built a miniature city, and the model was filmed walking round it.

3 A It's quite obvious that it isn't real.
  B I know that, but it talks and moves just like a real one.
  A That's true, but only when you see it in close-up.
  B And you never actually see both of them in close-up at the same time.
  A So how did they do the long shots?
  B It's just a lifelike plastic model which is stuck on to the actor's shoulder.

Unit 15, Stage two, 5

A I think all private cars should be banned. At the moment they're polluting the atmosphere and causing chaos in towns and cities. Even motorways can't cope. People should travel …

B In my opinion nuclear power stations should be closed. They're too expensive to run and, whatever the politicians and scientists say, they're dangerous. We don't want any more Chernobyls. I think more money should be spent on alternative forms of energy, like …

C If you ask me, nothing should be done. I think people are making a lot of fuss about nothing. It's all media hype. I mean, every time you turn the television on, there's someone saying the world's going to end tomorrow. I think people …

D At the moment we're wasting valuable resources. It's quite simple: all our rubbish should be recycled. It certainly shouldn't be buried or …

E As I see it, the people who cause the pollution – I mean industries and individuals – should be fined for …

Unit 15, Stage two, 6

A I think all private cars should be banned. At the moment they're polluting the atmosphere and causing chaos in towns and cities. Even motorways can't cope. People should travel by public transport like buses or trains.

B In my opinion nuclear power stations should be closed. They're too expensive to run and, whatever the politicians and scientists say, they're dangerous. We don't want any more Chernobyls. I think more money should be spent on alternative forms of energy, like solar energy and wind power.

C If you ask me, nothing should be done. I think people are making a lot of fuss about nothing. It's all media hype. I mean, every time you turn the television on, there's someone saying the world's going to end tomorrow. I think people are worrying too much.

D At the moment we're wasting valuable resources. It's quite simple: all our rubbish should be recycled. It certainly shouldn't be buried or burnt.

E As I see it, the people who cause the pollution – I mean industries and individuals – should be fined for the damage they do.

Unit 15, Stage two, 8

1 I think it's terrible that people dump their rubbish at the roadsides.
2 This waste in landfill sites soon pollutes water supplies and soil.
3 Eighteen per cent of household rubbish is metal or plastic.
4 Thirty per cent is paper and cardboard.
5 Pollution is a danger to all forms of wildlife as well as to human beings and plants.

IRREGULAR VERBS

Infinitive	Past Tense	Past Participle	Infinitive	Past Tense	Past Participle
be	was/were	been	lie	lay	lain
beat	beat	beaten	light	lighted, lit	lighted, lit
become	became	become	lose	lost	lost
begin	began	begun	make	made	made
bend	bent	bent	mean	meant	meant
bet	bet, betted	bet, betted	meet	met	met
bite	bit	bitten	pay	paid	paid
blow	blew	blown	put	put	put
break	broke	broken	read /ri:d/	read /red/	read /red/
bring	brought	brought	ride	rode	ridden
build	built	built	ring	rang	rung
burn	burnt, burned	burnt, burned	rise	rose	risen
buy	bought	bought	run	ran	run
catch	caught	caught	say	said	said
choose	chose	chosen	see	saw	seen
come	came	come	sell	sold	sold
cost	cost	cost	send	sent	sent
cut	cut	cut	set	set	set
dig	dug	dug	sew	sewed	sewn, sewed
do	did	done	shake	shook	shaken
draw	drew	drawn	shoot	shot	shot
dream	dreamt, dreamed	dreamt, dreamed	shine	shone	shone
drink	drank	drunk	show	showed	shown, showed
drive	drove	driven	shut	shut	shut
eat	ate	eaten	sing	sang	sung
fall	fell	fallen	sink	sank	sunk
feed	fed	fed	sit	sat	sat
feel	felt	felt	sleep	slept	slept
fight	fought	fought	slide	slid	slid
find	found	found	smell	smelt, smelled	smelt, smelled
fly	flew	flown	speak	spoke	spoken
forget	forgot	forgotten	spell	spelt, spelled	spelt, spelled
freeze	froze	frozen	spend	spent	spent
get	got	got	spill	spilt, spilled	spilt, spilled
give	gave	given	stand	stood	stood
go	went	gone	steal	stole	stolen
grow	grew	grown	stick	stuck	stuck
hang	hung	hung	sweep	swept	swept
have	had	had	swim	swam	swum
hear	heard	heard	swing	swung	swung
hide	hid	hidden	take	took	taken
hit	hit	hit	teach	taught	taught
hold	held	held	tear	tore	torn
hurt	hurt	hurt	tell	told	told
keep	kept	kept	think	thought	thought
know	knew	known	throw	threw	thrown
lay	laid	laid	understand	understood	understood
lead	led	led	wake	woke	woken
learn	learnt, learned	learnt, learned	wear	wore	worn
leave	left	left	win	won	won
lend	lent	lent	work	worked	worked
let	let	let	write	wrote	written

INDEX

The page numbers in **bold** type indicate Language review pages.

a   19, 22, 128, **131**
Ability   89, 94
able to   89, **94**
Adjectives
   with *-able*   128
   comparative   7, **13**
   with *-ing* and *-ed*   45
   with *-ish*   5
   order of   30, **32**
   possessive   **86**
   superlative   110, 111, **113**
Adverbs of frequency   7, **12**
Advice   106, 107, **113**
Age   12
Agreeing and disagreeing   56, **58**
any (and *some*)   79, **85**
Arrangements   74, **77**
Articles   19, **22**, 128, **131**

can   89, 90, **94**
Certainty and uncertainty   115, **122**
Comparative adjectives   7, **13**
Compound nouns   137
Compound pronouns   52, **58**
Conditional, First   110, **113**
Conditional, Second   125, **131**
could   119, **122**
Countable nouns   80, **85**

Definite article   (19, **22**), 26, **32**, 128, **131**
Describing objects   29, 30, **32**
Describing people   5, 6
Direct speech   97, **103**
Disagreeing (and agreeing)   56, **58**
Dislikes (and likes)   37, **39**
do (and *make*)   75, **77**

enough (and *too*)   91
everybody and *nobody*   52, **58**
excuses   101
feel   115
First Conditional   110, **113**
for and *since*   64, **68**
forget (and *remember*)   17, **22**
Frequency adverbs   7, **12**
Future
   with *going to*   74, **77**
   with *will*   71, **77**
Future Continuous   71, **77**

get phrasal verbs   91
going to   71, 74 **77**

have/had to   90, 92, **94**
have got to   **94**
hear and *see*   45, **49**
How long?   64, 65, **68**
How much/many?   80, **85**
How often?   7, **12**

if   see **Conditionals**
Imperatives   **113**
Indefinite article   (19, **22**), 128, **131**
Intentions   74, **77**
Irregular verbs   **22**

keep   100

Likes and dislikes   37, **39**
look   7, **13**
lot of, a   **85**

make and *do*   75, **77**
many   **85**
may and *might*   115, 116, 119, **122**
Measurements   83, **86**

might (and *may*)   115, 116, 119, **122**
Modals   see *must*, *need*, etc.
Money expressions   125
most   118, **122**
much   **85**
must/mustn't   92, **94**

Nationality   6
Necessity   90, **94**
need/needn't   92, **94**
nobody (and *everybody*)   52, **58**
Nouns
   countable and uncountable   80, **85**
   compound   137
Numbers and statistics   15, **86**, 109

Object pronouns   83, **86**
Obligations   128, **131**
Offering help   72
Opinions asking for and giving   34, **39**, 52, **58**, 137, **140**
Order of adjectives   30, **32**
ought to   128, **131**

Passive verbs   133, 136, **140**
Past Continuous   45, **49**
Past Simple   16, 19, **22**, 63
Past time phrases   16, **22**
Permission   **94**
Plans   74, **77**
Possessive adjectives   **86**
Possessive pronouns   82, **86**
Possibilities *can, could, may, might*   **94**, 119, **122**
Predictions   71
Preferences   39
Prepositions   8, 16, 25, **32**, 73
Present Continuous   9, **13**

page 158   INDEX

INDEX

Present Perfect Continuous
  65, 66, **68**
Present Perfect Simple
  43, **49**, 62-4, **68**
Present Simple 6, 9, **12**
Prices 80, **85**
Pronouns
  compound 52, **58**
  object 83, **86**
  possessive 82, **86**
  you, we, they with general meaning 53, **58**
Pronunciation see below

Quantities **85**
Questions 44, 65, 109

Question tags 64, **68**
quite and *rather* 6, **12**

rather 6, **12**
Recommendations and obligations 128, **131**
remember and *forget* 17, **22**
Reported speech 97, 100, **103**
Reporting verbs 100, **103**

Second Conditional 125, **131**
see (and *hear*) 45, **49**
Sequencers 42, 45, **49**
should 128, **131**
since and *for* 64, **68**
some and *any* 79, **85**

Suggestions 34, **39**
Superlative adjectives
  110, 111, **113**

take phrasal verbs 20
the (19, **22**), 26, **32**, 128, **131**
too (and *enough*) 91
Uncertainty (and certainty)
  115, **122**
Uncountable nouns 80, **85**
used to **22**

Value 82, **85**
will 71, **77**
would see **Conditionals**

Pronunciation Index

Contractions 129
Contrastive stress 80
Homophones 37
Intonation
  questions 42
  question tags 64, **68**
Past Simple *-ed* ending 16
Present Simple *-s* ending 6
Rhythm 92

Schwa 52
Stress
  compound nouns 137
  contrastive 80
  key words 25, 111, 116
  long words 25, 62
  new information 116

Vowels, diphthongs and consonants
  / ɪ / and / iː / 30
  / ʊ / and / ɔː / 107
  / ə / 52
  / ɪə / and / ɛə / 34
  / b / and / v / 98
  / ŋ / 73

Thomas Nelson and Sons Ltd
Nelson House   Mayfield Road
Walton-on-Thames   Surrey
KT12 5PL   UK

51 York Place
Edinburgh
EH1 3JD   UK

Thomas Nelson (Hong Kong) Ltd
Toppan Building 10/F
22A Westlands Road
Quarry Bay   Hong Kong

© Simon Haines and Simon Brewster 1991

First published by Thomas Nelson and Sons Ltd 1991

ISBN 0-17-555921-X

NPN 9 8 7 6 5 4 3 2 1

All Rights Reserved. This publication is protected in the United Kingdom by the Copyright Act 1956 and in other countries by comparable legislation. No part of it may be reproduced or recorded by any means without the permission of the publisher. This prohibition extends (with certain very limited exceptions) to photocopying and similar processes, and written permission to make a copy or copies must therefore be obtained from the publisher in advance. It is advisable to consult the publisher if there is any doubt regarding the legality of any proposed copying.

Printed in Hong Kong

Acknowledgements

The publishers are grateful to the following for permission to reproduce copyright material:

The Sunday Times for the article on John and David Suchet, © Times Newspapers Ltd. 1988 (page 7), and 'Gabor Plans a Gourmet Life in Jail', © Times Newspapers Ltd. 1989 (page 96)

Penguin Books Ltd. for the extract from *The Great Railway Bazaar* by Paul Theroux (page 27)

Just Seventeen magazine for the interview with Jason Donovan (page 36)

Punch magazine for the cartoons by McLachlan (page 40) and Pugh (page 123)

Early Times for the articles: 'Leeds Newsboy Earns Praise in Bomb Action' by Simon Walsh (page 41), and 'Suffering from the School Bus Smokers' (page 53)

Newsweek for 'Into the 21st Century', redrawn by Julia Osorno from an original by Ib Ohlsson (page 70)

United Media for the two Peanuts cartoons by Schulz, © United Features Syndicate, Inc. 1987 & 1988 (page 72)

J Sainsbury plc for the adapted till receipt (page 78)

The Colchester Express for the article 'Take some French Leave for Bargains' by Diane Firmin (page 81)

The Face magazine for the article 'Heavy Metal' (page 83)

Scoop News and Music for the extract from 'Slot Machines - Could You Get Addicted?' (page 84), and the article 'Riddle of the Rings' (page 118)

Channel 4 Television from the extracts from *Baka: People of the Rain Forest* (page 88)

The Daily Mail for the article 'We're Just Too Worried to Have Fun on Holiday' by Willy Newlands (page 108)

Random Century group for the extract from *Prevention Is Better* by Dr Andrew Stanway, published by Century (page 110)

Japan National Tourist Organization for the text 'Visiting Japan' (page 127)

Woman magazine for the texts adapted from 'How Do You Doodle?' by Patricia Marne (page 141)

Every effort has been made to trace owners of copyright, but if any omissions can be rectified, the publishers will be pleased to make the necessary arrangements.

Photographs

Phil Agland   page 88;   Allsport pages 33 (2), 34, 114 (6);   Art Directors pages 35, 109;   Penni Bickle page 21;   B.F.I. Stills page 120;   Camera Press page 127;   John Urling Clark pages 6, 49;   Bruce Coleman pages 31, 87;   Greg Evans pages 9 (2), 10, 24, 25 (2), 26, 33 (3), 34, 59 (4), 74, 109, 114;   Mary Evans pages 117 (3), 118, 119 (3);   Amanda Gillis page 59;   Sally & Richard Greenhill page 59;   V.K. Guy page 61;   Robert Harding pages 59, 109 (3), 127 (2), 129, 130;   The Hulton Picture Library pages 14, 15 (3), 20;   The Image Bank pages 23, 27, 44, 59, 62, 81, 83, 114, 127, 135;   The Kobal Collection pages 4, 9 (2), 120, 132 (8), 134;   Madam Tussaudes page 9;   The National Trust page 44;   Planet Earth pages 60, 87 (5);   Chris Ridgers Photography pages 5, 29, 33 (4), 34, 50, 56, 57, 78, 104 (5), 107, 109, 111 (2), 124, 134;   Rex Features pages 4 (3), 36, 46 (2), 47, 96, 120;   Das pages 5 (3), 33, 104 (2), 111 (2), 124 (5);   Tony Stone Associates pages 38, 126;   *The Sunday Times* page 7;   Seaphot page 87;   *The Yorkshire Evening Post* page 41;   Zefa pages 9, 25

Illustrations

Angela Barnes   pages 30, 37, 54, 55, 79, 93, 128, 139
Peter Byatt   pages 5, 11, 16, 18, 27, 28, 48, 51, 55, 56, 69, 71, 101
Jo Dennis   pages 8, 53, 80, 89, 92, 112
Trevor Dunton (Steven Wells Illustration Agency)   pages 43, 45, 46, 70, 73, 75, 82, 86, 100, 121, 137
Susannah English (Steven Wells Illustration Agency)   pages 9, 43, 63, 65, 90, 91, 98, 103
Yvonne Gay   page 84
Pauline King   pages 102, 116
Julia Osorno   pages 18, 23, 28, 39, 70, 88, 95, 126